Nice  Said

The Great Gamble is an incredible guide for exploring the question "Does God Exist?" Jim Bryson engages the intellect but with heart and soul. Jim's joyful, dare I say irreverent, approach helps disarm our dogmas and instead helps us wrestle with the evidence without judgement. Every agnostic should read this book and let it challenge and delight you as you reexamine the central question. Jim's lighthearted yet profound way of working through the ageless debates may lead you to a great gamble.

Dr. Timothy Hamon
CEO – Christian International Ministries Network
President of CI School of Theology

I enjoyed taking on The Great Gamble to see where the author put his chips. With wit, skill and clarity Jim presents a clear pathway toward the evidence that if there is a visible Creation to experience then we with integrity can no longer deny the opportunity to also experience the Creator. The author provides all the "breadcrumbs" a reader needs to follow the trail and discover for themselves both the Forest and Trees. The only thing keeping anyone from this adventure is the desire to go.

Paul Mackie, Teacher, Speaker and Spiritual Father
Author of *Equip, Empower, Engage*
and *Becoming What We Behold*

Jim Bryson is my editor. He is a very gifted writer, and I have personally encouraged him to write his own books. I am amazed at his ability to put words together that create a reality that cannot be ignored. He can get from A to Z, more easily than the rest of us because he ignores most of the letters in the alphabet. I'm not saying he doesn't use them; I'm saying they aren't letters anymore, but merge into concepts, ideas, and logic that morph the English alphabet into a path leading to a place you've never been. He is a wordsmith. When you walk through each chapter, you will grasp the concepts like a hungry man who suddenly finds himself in a ripe apple orchard. Take the journey with Jim. The Great Gamble is worth the gamble. You will be enriched by its contents.

Regina Shank, Apostolic Leader and CEO
Global Transformation International
Founder, Feeding Incorporated

"The truth is, God needs no introduction, he only needs an opening." I love this statement Jim Bryson makes in this book. In my own quest for purpose and the meaning of life, I did not believe there was a God much less one who was concerned about me. I discovered I only needed to be willing. I did not need to obtain a certain amount of knowledge or know any Bible stories. Neither did I need to obtain a certain level of goodness in my behavior. The longing that is inside each of us to be loved and valued drew me to the only one who could love me perfectly, not holding what I did or said against me. Our journey to discover and then to know God is deeply personal and unique. The questions Jim Bryson presents in this book and the ideas to ponder are a beautiful journey of discovery if we choose to go on that journey. He only needs an opening.

Joe Nicola
Author of *Ekklesia; the Government of the Kingdom of Heaven,*
and *Now Who Are You?*

I like Jim's writing style, the stories and the humor. He's thoughtful and articulate (almost meticulous). He wrestles through the logic of God's existence in pro's and con's that we all walk through. Jim shows us God isn't just a concept, a theology, or a doctrine. He has a heart and loves relationships. The final straw in our resistance breaks with an experience of the heart – that's when it all makes sense. He's alive!

John Garfield, Teacher, Speaker, Engineer
Author of *Releasing Kings for Marketplace Ministry,*
From Desire to Destiny,
Seers and Doers
Intentional Reformation

Jim Bryson's book displays an incredible knack for evaluating God's existence in an unusual style to the confused, skeptical and curious by deftly using detailed research, humor and compassion in a way that makes you enjoy the search for God."

Rufus M. Friday
Former News Media President & Publisher
Lexington (KY) Herald-Leader

In a word, WOW!

This book was written for me and every other person struggling to understand God. I really enjoyed reading it. It's made me think deeper and open my mind (and heart) to the possibility of God.

Col. Adam Bryson, USMC
Stuttgart, Germany

"The valley rich in things we cannot fathom." When a familiar concept rushes to the brain in fresh language, the reader is hooked. With the relentless precision of a seasoned professional engineer, Jim Bryson draws in Christians to examine their long-held beliefs, agnostics to wonder if they have misunderstood Christians, and atheists to question if he might just have a case. In a style that shifts from vivid illustrations to urgent imperatives, *The Great Gamble* flows through the reader with prophetic clarity.

A book for our times!

Neil Paul, BA, MA
Teacher of English Literature (retired)
Community Lay Preacher and Poet

The Great Gamble

Gamble

An Empirical Argument
For the Modern Agnostic

Jim Bryson

Spring Mill Publishing
Sharpsburg, Maryland

Copyright

The Great Gamble
An Empirical Argument
For the Modern Agnostic

by Jim Bryson

Published by SPRING MILL PUBLISHING

Sharpsburg, Maryland 21782 USA

Graphics by Amani Hanson

Dedication

TO NEIL PAUL, my cherished friend, poet, teacher, Shakespearian scholar and occasional debate partner over matters of theology, poetry and all things Canadian. Neil, your gentle spirit blanketed my rocky American soul. I came to rely on your patient well-being, your curious phrasing of the English language you loved, your stories of the students you taught in the heart of Ontario's farm country, your personal history of the friends and neighbors surrounding you, and most of all, your reason for being—taking every day as a gift.

Listening to you was like reading a book so eager to be read that it bent and flowed to fit the listener's ear. I miss your calm acceptance, even as I blaze forth to light the world. I hear your voice in the tranquil distance, your quizzical smile offering one more story before I ride off into the sunset. Alas, it was you who rode off first, eh?

Here's to the other side where all great poets return, all theologians have a good laugh on themselves, and loved ones never again leave their friends.

Acknowledgments

I'D LIKE TO THANK the many people who give input on this book. It was with great trepidation that I inched further and further out onto this thin limb of theological discourse. I realized, from a lifetime of editing other people's work, that my thoughts could be construed as "out there" for most conventional thinkers. But the people who matter most are those who have read the manuscript and returned changed.

Today in modern culture, we are arguing about God in ways that make no sense. Indeed, we are not even arguing; we are shouting, posturing, judging and ultimately ignoring all other sides to this great quest—deciding on God's existence.

I want to thank all my endorsers and the many more whose comments impacted these pages. No man is an island, though occasionally we get swamped by the tides.

Contents

All my gods died in Vietnam...

Sheriff Lewis Cody–*Shepherd of the Wolves*

by William S. Slusher

Introduction

I BELIEVE IN GOD, and I realize that many people do not. There is an atheism that seems to be in vogue these days, and there are many people with agnostic perspectives—they simply don't know, they don't see the relevance of finding out, or they prefer their higher power to remain abstract.

I don't blame them. I get it. Ayn Rand, the founder of a philosophy called Objectivism, put it well: Without evidence of God, there is no rational reason to believe in God.

She's right.

My belief in God is anything but irrational. I can think of a hundred other things about me that are irrational—my fears, my phobias, my passion for motorcycles, and the belief that the Washington Football Team will one day have a winning season.

Yeah, I'm one of those.

Yet my belief in God is based on experience, the evidence of nearly 50 years of wrestling with all that life throws at us and coming back time after time to the one the enduring attribute of my existence—that God exists and he loves us.

But that's just me. It may not be you. In fact, I dearly hope it's not, because you're the reason I wrote this. Atheists, agnostics, the I-don't-really-care people, are some of my closest friends. They are good people. I love them and they love me—mostly. They are men and women who work hard, care for their families, live productive and often sacrificial lives, struggle with shortcomings while refining their strengths. They are the planks of society; their core values are the moral bedrock of all we consider civilized. They hold staunch opinions while remaining open to differing views. They are not easily drawn out, yet they don't shy from conflict when necessary. They are good, good people.

And late at night, when the house is quiet and sleep beckons, they may close their eyes and let a glimmer of light through the shade drawn over their hearts and wonder...if only for a moment...if there is something more...something out there waiting to be discovered...just as they themselves are waiting for discovery.

It's our secret yearnings that need attending, the ones we dare not believe for risk of disappointment. I can accept that I'll never fly like a bird, for example, so it doesn't haunt me. Then a peregrine falcon swoops down from the sky, roosts in a nearby tree and stares at the horizon. And just like that, the dream revives and I yearn to soar with him.

Many people dream of something beyond themselves, something benevolent and powerful. But they rationalize away the yearning and get on with life the best they can...until hope comes to roost above them and their dreams revive.

I can offer evidence for God's existence, but I can't prove it to you. You have to do that on your own. But I'd like to show you how to look for evidence—how to perceive it and evaluate it—and how to know when it soars overhead.

I want to reach your dreams.

If you stay with me through these pages, you'll experience the gradual development of an over-arching pitch. It will take several chapters. I'm not shy of words. But I promise to keep you interested. Bored people don't read for long and they comprehend even less.

We'll look at who we are—that part of ourselves that must be engaged to consider God's existence. Then we'll evaluate what constitutes evidence. Finally, we'll look at what has led others to their conclusions about God's existence. The goal, as stated, is a quest, not a destination. It's a map, a path, one that I travel along with many others.

If there is one universal truth, it's that our understanding of truth is always evolving. It's the natural cycle of living and dying, the art of decay, the dissolution of all we thought we knew to nourish the next season of life.

Thank you for your time.

> *It's not some message written in the dark,*
> *Or some truth that no one's seen,*
> *It's a little bit of everything.*

Taylor Goldsmith – *A Little Bit of Everything*

1

A God Who...

Have you heard of the dyslexic agnostic insomniac? He stayed up all night wondering about the existence of Dog.

AN INTERESTING CONVERSATION occurs frequently in my life. Because I am known in some circles as a believer in God, and I also happen to be a good listener, I often hear people's take on God. It typically goes like this:

"I don't believe in God."

"Oh really? Why not?"

"I can't believe in a God who lets babies starve, animals suffer and people slaughter themselves in senseless wars."

I usually pause at that point because I understand what they're saying. More importantly, I know why they are saying it. When they collect their breath, I offer the following:

"I don't believe in that God either."

When the surprise hits their face, I add:

"The God I believe in is not responsible for babies starving, animals suffering, wars inflicted on people, or any of the host of evils we all face. In fact, the God I serve is opposed to these things. And if we followed him closer, we would see less evil in this world."

Now, what happened here? Our discussion was not really about believing in God. That was the surface issue. We were really talking about *who* God is—our definition of God. By refusing to believe in God because we see babies starving, the person was saying "God is responsible for babies starving." A variant of that would be "God is responsible for *allowing* babies to starve." Either way, the assumption is that God can do something about this evil and for whatever reason, he chooses not to.

But notice too, that the conversation has another interesting twist. To say "I can't believe in a God who..." requires a deeper definition of *believe*.

BELIEVE

If something is real, our unbelief does not affect its existence. I could debate gravity's existence from atop the Sears Tower in Chicago, but no matter how firmly I hold to my disbelief, I will still have mere seconds to learn to fly before the sudden impact makes gravity's presence known with extreme prejudice.

Likewise, I could choose to not believe in my brother's existence, but that doesn't mean that he would vanish. The ink on his birth certificate is not going to disappear when I declare him non-existent, and neither is the mess he made in my garage when he changed the oil in his truck. The guy still exists, no matter how I feel about him at the moment.

Reality is that which, when you stop believing in it, doesn't go away.

Philip K. Dick

While most of us are not foolish enough to debate the forces of nature or the presence of annoying relatives, we seem to have no problem negating the existence of God simply on the basis that this being does not meet our expectations. Can belief in God really be that simple? Or is there something more?

Looking closer, we see that the phrase "I can't believe in a God who..." really means something more. *Believe*, in this context, is less about God's existence and more about our acknowledgement, reliance and allegiance to said God. Fundamentally, the person declaring their refusal to believe in God is really saying that God, as they understand him, fails to meet their expectations. In actuality, they are revealing something about themselves, not God. They are speaking from their yearning for something worth believing in, something greater than themselves, something worth acknowledging, relying on, and aligning to. As such, they are speaking from their need for something beyond what they consider to be God.

If I declared: "The only thing Ford trucks stand for is *'Found On the Road Dead,'*" and further said: "I would never own one in a million years," you might label me a Ford hater (or I could be working for Elon Musk), but you would also know something more significant about me—that deep down inside, I care about trucks.

Most likely, my passionate dislike for Ford trucks comes from a greater passion to find something reliable to get me, my tools and my dogs up and down the road. In my negative declaration against Ford, I am presenting evidence of my search for a truck I can believe in, something worthy of my investment.

It's the same with God. The most vehement critic, the most vocal opponent, the staunchest opposer to the existence of God is someone who has obviously thought and felt a great deal about God. Their resistance to the existence of God comes from a place of intense longing, a place uninhabited by something sufficiently real to believe in.

Obviously, it's important to them or they wouldn't be resisting so strenuously. They are looking for something to believe in. They are looking for the truth.

DEFINE YOUR TERMS

"God is...you know...GOD! Duh!"

Before we can determine the existence of anything, we first must know what we are looking for. We have to define it. Without a clear definition, we don't know what to look for, how to look for it, or even if we've found it.

This is true in our search for God. How we define God has everything to do with the results of our quest. If I define God as a Honda ST1300 motorcycle, then I can say with certainty that God exists. In fact, he lives in my garage.

Everyone has a definition of God, but not everyone can articulate their definition. The word "God" flows through our thoughts and conversations so easily that it has become a common term, accepted without examination. God has become Kleenex for nose tissue, Xerox for photocopying machines, Dallas Cowboys for perennially losing football teams. If I hit my thumb with a hammer and cry "God-----!" it's clear that my definition of God includes someone to blame for my pain. If I cry "Oh my God!" it's clear that God ranks up there with my greatest amazement.

Nobody thinks about who or what God is. We just accept the meaning implied in the context of the discussion.

THE GREAT CONVERSATION

Of course, everybody's definition of God is different, although no definition of God is original. In a world possessed by a singular search for its identity, purpose and fulfillment, a great conversation ripples through our population. Are we alone or not? Is anybody up there? To what extent are we visited if indeed something greater exists at all?

Whether we know it or not, we are constantly seeking God, even the idea of God, and weighing the evidence.

We hear of God in church, in popular music, in discussions about fate, randomness of life, the future and the past. We curse God when things go awry. Athletes salute God when they score and kneel when companions are injured. Soldiers commit themselves to divine providence before charging into withering fire and scream God's name as they cry for help. Rulers align themselves with God as a divine mandate before the people. Even a dictator like Napoleon, who famously said "God is on the side with the best artillery," draws from the concept of a divine intervener. Certainly, he intended it to be a wry declaration of the non-involvement of God, but would this sardonic observation mean anything if the concept of God was not in the common lexicon in the first place? Clearly, he was making fun of the prevalent idea that God decided the outcome of battles.

So, what are people saying about God? What are they thinking and feeling? What do you hear?

God is alive.

God is dead.

God is a figment of the imagination.

God is returning on 15 December 2035 at 11:59 pm.

Our first quest, then, in determining if God exists, is arriving at the truth about who (or what) God is.

The truth.

Are we looking for what's really there? Or are we looking to confirm what we already believe? Validation is easy. Truth requires a little more effort.

Whether you think you know God or you are certain there is no God, I hope to lead you on a journey to develop your methodology for determining the existence or non-existence of God.

2

What and Why?

IN OUR SEARCH FOR TRUTH, we cannot take anything for granted.

The search for evidence of God's existence requires similar skills as getting to know our fellow man. The ability to go past our surface impressions of the concept of God is the same that we use for our friends and neighbors, our workmates, business partners, and of course, our loved ones. Looking past the surface is the key to uncovering truth.

Have you ever been in a position where you thought you knew someone well, only to find out later, perhaps as the relationship deepened, that you did not know them at all? That the qualities you based your admiration or affection on were merely what they wanted you to see or what you wanted to see in them? Of course you have. You're human after all.

You never knew what I loved in you
I don't know what you loved in me
Maybe the picture of somebody
You were hoping I might be

11

Jackson Browne – *Late for the Sky*

Now go back to our example of someone saying: "I can't believe in a God who..." Recall how they really meant something entirely different. At their core, they really cared about the conditions they were blaming God for, and obviously, they had some belief structure in place to reject God in the first place.

WHAT AND WHY

When I listen to someone express an opinion, I care little for *what* they are saying. I'm much more interested in *why* they are saying it. The *why* tells me the reason for their thinking. It reveals what is behind the opinion. Often, what is behind the opinion is a person wanting to be understood.

"The President sucks!"

"Got it. You think the president sucks."

"No....he *really* does."

"Really? Why?"

"OMG! Where to start? Because he *does*...that's why!"

Most people can't tell you why they think what they do. They don't understand themselves well enough to articulate the forces driving their viewpoints. Yet this is key to deciding if God exists or not.

To understand the *why*, as in why they think that way, you have to understand the person. Where in the person's being does the opinion arise from? Their thoughts and feelings are a start, but the real drivers come from a deeper place. Consider:

Their mind: reading, learning, education, logic, values, standards, examples.

Their heart: joys, sorrows, triumphs, failures, fears, dreams, aspirations.

Their self-image: confidence, focus, cultural standing.

Their influencers: heroes, villains, mentors, tormentors, inspirations.

Their inner condition: resilient, wounded, whole, broken.

You see, a lot is happening in the briefest of opinions...if you are perceptive and motivated enough to uncover it. True compassion, and hence enduring love, arises from the intimate experience of the person(s) involved.

As we consider the existence of God, we have to think deeper than our surface impressions of God—what we've been taught, what we have concluded based in fleeting observation. We have to dig a little deeper into the concept we are trying to evaluate. We have to begin to evaluate where our opinions of God (existent or non-existent) come from. We have to understand truth.

BEYOND THE SURFACE

"What is truth?" is more than the plea of a confused man staring into the eyes of truth itself. It is a life-long quest. It is a river that flows around us and through us.

Two things will kill our experience of truth:

- Assuming we have all the answers.

- Assuming the answers will never change.

The search for the truth about God's existence is an intensely personal journey. It cannot be satisfied through platitudes or mass marketing campaigns.

Jesus freaks out in the street
Handing tickets out for God

Bernie Taupin

As I often say to the well-meaning missionaries who ring my doorbell and offer pamphlets to persuade me to their perspective: "The engagement you are promoting is deeply personal, so much so that cold-calling a stranger seems to defeat all that a meaningful relationship with God purports to offer. Like a mail-order bride arriving on a doorstep, I think we should get to know one another a little first before we talk about moving into one another's heart-spaces."

That usually ends the encounter.

Fact is, we are not looking for a quick-fix answer or something to watch during the commercials. There's much more at stake here.

Truth is not about answers. It's about flow, a journey, a river. Truth doesn't stand still. It flows into your life, surrounds you and continues on. It flows on with or without you. It's an irresistible force for good, but you must remove the impediments for it to flow through you.

Stagnant water is soon stale.

The life is in the flow.

We have to understand truth...about who we are and who God might be. And this will require time and discovery.

3

Our Whole Beings

OUR SEARCH FOR GOD begins with a definition, not one that is fixed in stone, but a strawman, a starting point, a spirit brooding over darkness waiting for light to appear. That spirit is our own.

As we find clues—more importantly, as we decide what we will accept as clues—we find ourselves in a quest for the knowledge of God.

The knowledge of anything starts with accepting the possibility of its existence. This acceptance is based on evidence.

- I never suspected that germs existed until I caught a cold.
- I never dreamed that poverty existed until I couldn't feed my children.
- I never knew love existed until she smiled.
- I never thought of God until I looked up.

As we learn *how to determine* if God exists, proving his existence or lack thereof will be relatively simple.

HEART AND MIND

The search for God's existence is not a sterile one. We are not merely acquiescing to a conclusion based on mental reasoning. While that may appeal to a finely tuned mind, it's duplicitous. If I search with only a narrow aspect of my being—my mind—I have already restricted the means by which evidence can reach me. I've stacked the deck to get the results I expected all along. My mind becomes a filter of my choosing.

Requiring that God's existence meet an intellectual test says, at its core, that God's existence can be found through the intellect alone.

The issue is that the human being is an elaborate structure. We think on one level, feel on another level, and make decisions on yet a third level, each deeper than the previous level. By the time you think it, you will have already felt it, and that feeling has come up from the core of your being—the place of awareness. We have hearts and minds and something deeper. Scientists have a highly developed technical term for it. They call it "gut."

The part of the brain that controls inspiration and vision is called the limbic brain. It controls all of our feelings, but doesn't have any capacity for language. This is why we trust our gut, even though why we do that can't be put in words.

Simon Sinek

Listen, we are more than minds. We are hearts. We are spirits. We are guts. We are history and future—the product of what has come before us and the foundation of what will come after us. If our search for God is anything less than an all-consuming quest of our entire beings, it is doomed.

I know...I know...some think themselves intellectuals driven by reason. If something can't be proven logically, it doesn't exist. I've known a few of these people—I was one for a time—and here's what I learned. You can only ignore your heart for so long until reality asserts itself.

Let's be honest. Let's seek truth with integrity. Let's search with accuracy. Let's examine God's existence using our whole beings.

WE ARE THE SEARCH

As an engineer who helped design and build some of the most complex facilities in the world, I constantly struggled to understand what was happening with a system I was trying to troubleshoot. I learned early on that "it's broke" is not a very helpful assessment of the situation.

Still, it's a start.

Effective troubleshooting requires data—the best data available. Consequently, the quest for data became a struggle for the most accurate measurements. I needed to know everything about the systems I was working on: the pressure, temperature, vibration, weight, speed, mass, voltage and power consumption. When I could describe the system in measurable parameters, I could more easily diagnose its problems and fix them. Without instruments capable of accurate measurement and analysis, I was running blind and my search was futile.

19

In addition to my measurements, I needed to know the system's history. How was it designed, constructed and started? Had it broken down before? What happened when it did?

Finally, it was crucial that I understood what the system was designed for—its intended function. I needed to know what a properly operating system looked like. Was it intended to filter gasses from a coal-fired boiler? Reheat steam for a turbine? Haul copper ore from a deep rock mine? Store solar heat like a battery? When I knew what the system was supposed to do (i.e., its definition), I was well on my way to diagnosing and fixing the issues preventing it from working properly.

Our search for evidence of God's existence is no different. Our instrumentation has to be good—the best there is—or our results will be suspect. The only thing worse than false data is skewed data—partially true, partially false. Further, we have to know what we are looking for just like the performance objectives in machine systems.

When it comes to the search for God's existence, we are the instrumentation. We were dropped into this world equipped with sensors that tell us what's happening around us. We all know our five senses: sight, touch, sound, smell and taste. We know that wind blows, winter rain soaks our clothes, the ground shakes, fire burns, seawater salts our lips, and our neighbor is a heavy metal fan. We know what to bury and what to dig up, what to eat and what to throw away.

And yet our awareness goes beyond our physical senses.

We sense things, hear things, see things that have no physical explanation. A painting speaks to us. A song transports us. A sunrise beckons us and a spring morning jerks us from our bed and puts a hoe in our hands before we smell breakfast.

We know when someone is around a corner, when a smile is a dagger, if tears are real. We know when our mother in Omaha is about to call (or when we should call her).

We know love, hate, pain, joy, despair and exhilaration. We feel loneliness and fulfillment. We embrace purpose. We revel in love.

I know my children love me. How? Because they always come to me for money? Well...yeah. But more so, I feel it. Know what I mean? My heart sings when my daughter hugs me. I feel proud when my son admires a job I did. "Nice work Dad. You didn't blow anything up this time."

I know when my wife is happy with me and when she's livid. I sense this, you know? Like when pots fly through the air or the TV cable gets cut during the playoffs. (I guess I'm just tele-pathetic.)

These senses are not thoughts. They're not even emotions sometimes. Certainly, they inform our minds and hearts, but they're more. Something is driving them, something deeper arising from the core of our beings, making contact with others at the same level. Iron sharpens iron. Deep calls to deep. This is beyond logic or time or reason; more than four dimensions or five senses. It is human, the wholeness of who we are: body, soul and spirit.

21

We can't be anything less and expect to find evidence of God.

Our pursuit of God's existence is as good as we are. In the end, we are the means by which we will discover the truth.

WHO ARE YOU?

A belief in God's existence is not merely an excuse for endless debates around campfires. It is not fodder for fiery sermons flung from far pulpits. It is not a litmus test for assigning unbelievers to eternal flames and others to pearly gates. It is not a reason to love those we agree with and hate those we don't. Indeed, such debates have little to do with God and everything to do with ourselves.

We can't debate God's existence until we understand *what* we are looking for, *why* we are looking for it, and *how* we are looking for it. The key is this: The *what*, *why* and *how* all come from *who we are*.

As we work to accurately form any question, we systematically approach the answer. Declaring: "I'm hungry" doesn't satisfy anything. But asking: "What's for dinner?" comes a little closer.

Since you are reading this, chances are you have a question leading you on a quest—perhaps a doubt, a nagging thought, an ache, a wonderment, a hunger, an insight that there is more to life. Or maybe you're just fed up with idiotic Christians and their religious garbage.

I can't convince you of God's existence. And if I could sway you, it would only serve as evidence of my persuasive abilities, not the integrity of any argument. We are here to consider the evidence of God's existence and make up our own minds.

As with all things, it's the journey that proves the truth. One thing that binds human beings in harmony is that truth is no respecter of persons. Something is either true or not true regardless of who considers it. As such, truth comprises reality.

However, truth may appear non-existence if, in our individual experiences, we do not perceive it. If we lack an appreciation for what is presented as evidence, we will eventually fall prey to our ignorance of reality.

In the end, reality always wins. That's why it's called reality.

I can live blissfully unaware of germs until one of them makes me sick. I can be ignorant of auto maintenance until my car dies on the Autobahn. I can deny gravity until the sudden landing convinces me of my need for wings. Ignorance kills.

My people are destroyed from lack of knowledge.

Ancient Hebrew Text

Integrity means being open to possibilities even as we refuse to accept things for which we have no evidence. Our lack of evidence could mean that there is no God, or it could mean that we are ignorant of credible evidence for God's existence.

The truth is the truth. Our belief structure doesn't get to determine what is truth. It only determines what we are willing to accept.

Once you eliminate the impossible, whatever remains, no matter how improbable, must be the truth.

Sir Arthur Conan Doyle

The questioning of God's existence is entirely honorable. I trust an open-minded atheist more than a closed-minded theist. There is no shame in ignorance, only in the unwillingness to learn.

To know God, we have to know what we are looking for and what we are using to find him. If all we use is our minds, that sieve will not pass anything but logic. If all we use is our hearts, our conclusions will amount to mindless babble. If all we use is our gut, we will become baseless rogues inhabiting a self-made reality to the exclusion of all conflicting facts.

But if we use our whole beings in pursuit of the evidence—all our senses open to whatever we perceive—then maybe...just maybe...we'll be on to something true. Perception sharpens with use. Like a telescope, whatever we aim our focus toward becomes clearer.

Maybe we'll find God. Maybe we won't. But either way, we'll be able to sleep better at night for having tried. Right?

Before we get into our examination of God's existence, however, let's look at the concept of judgment, a necessary subject for any pursuit of truth, especially the truth about a subject for which everyone has an opinion or three.

4

Judgment

THE SEARCH FOR EVIDENCE of God's existence requires
being open to possibilities. We cannot learn anything if our
opinions on the subject are intractable. Judging an issue
before we have all the facts prejudices our outlook.

If you are truly seeking evidence for or against the
existence of God—the most important search you will ever
undertake—you owe it to yourself to suspend judgment and
open yourself to the possibility of new evidence.

Here is a brief essay on the subject of judgment that I
hope you find useful.

SUSPENDING JUDGMENT

From the bible, we read some interesting proverbs:

Judge not, lest you be judged.

And...

A spiritual person judges all things.

At first glance, these sayings might seem contradictory.
That is because they are. But contradictions are not a

problem in nature. How does the bumblebee fly? How does electricity work? How does my accountant balance my checkbook? Apparent contradictions make sense when we understand the principles behind them. When it comes to learning, to being open to new ideas, it's important to understand this principle.

Judgment is the end of knowledge and the beginning of ignorance.

Interesting word, *ignorance.* Its meaning has everything to do with context.

ig·no·rance /ˈignərəns/ noun: "lack of knowledge or information."

Notice that ignorance is not necessarily a negative. It simply means "lacking knowledge." For example, I lack any knowledge of brain surgery. (I tried once, but the Acme School of Brain Surgery burned down before they could mail my degree.) So, my ignorance is not a negative. People don't go around whispering:

"Jim is pretty ignorant when it comes to brain surgery."

"No! Really? I thought there was something creepy about him."

But let me walk into an operating room ready to cut open somebody's head and my ignorance will take on a whole new connotation.

"Get that ignoramus out of here!!!"

Here's a way to understand ignorance with respect to judgment.

Consider a courtroom. When a judge presides over a case, she has to keep an open mind. As opposing attorneys argue back and forth and witnesses give conflicting sides to a story, the judge must hear all the facts without bias. In so doing, she is in a mode of learning—the gathering of knowledge.

After the judge has heard all the evidence, she makes up her mind, and in a gravelly voice, says: "It is the judgment of this court that blah blah blah...", and on she goes for 45 minutes while both parties trade snide looks over the padded shoulders of their overpaid attorneys.

She then slams her gavel (or whatever it's called; I think she's killing cockroaches), and the parties involved must abide by her ruling.

Note that at judgment, at the time of ruling, the judge is finished hearing evidence. She has passed the realm of learning. She is now in the realm of not-learning. She does not consider any more evidence. She issues her ruling based on what she knows at that moment.

Now, if minutes after judgment, a new witness rushes into the courtroom screaming that they have evidence that could clear Party A or convict Party B, the judge will say: "Sorry. Just killed the cockroach. Next case!"

See? She will ignore any further information now that she has issued her judgment. In so doing, she has left the state of learning and entered the state of ignorance. Consider again:

Judgment is the end of knowledge and the beginning of ignorance.

Now, if she is a righteous judge, she will have gathered all the information available before issuing her ruling. In so doing, she will have remained in a non-judgmental state for as long as necessary – days, weeks, months, or years, as the case may be. In this non-judgmental state, she is able to gather information. In a judgmental state, however, she is not open to gathering new information.

Judge not, lest you....be judged.

Remaining in a non-judgmental state is necessary for learning, but it is not as easy as it sounds. Picture yourself a parent at home when your 6-year-old, Lisa, comes running through the door, face covered in blood.

"Mommy! Mommy! Billy kicked me in the face."

What's your first reaction? *Care for Lisa.*

What's your second reaction? *Kill Billy.*

What's your third reaction? *Who the heck is Billy??*

See, you have already made up your mind that what Lisa told you is true. You have judged. And in a moment – as soon as the tourniquet is applied and the EMT's arrive, you intend to carry out sentence on that miscreant Billy.

Note, however, that you are beyond learning, past the point of gathering information. And why not What more do you need? You have all the evidence: Lisa's bloody face, the identity of her assailant, and the fact that you are bigger than this Billy kid. Time to execute judgment!

It is only after you burst outside with guns a-blazing that you discover the gate to the neighbor's goat pen unlocked and a large Billy-goat contentedly munching grass (and smirking—you swear!). That's when it hits you. Lisa must have ignored your repeated warnings and gone after the goats again.

Guess what?

You were wrong.

How did this happen?

Ignorance.

What brought you to ignorance?

Judgment.

Often, we have little time for information gathering. We read the newspaper about some national event and call the Congressperson an idiot. We pass a slow driver on the road and call him a jerk. We see an "A" on our daughter's report card and declare her a genius.

Yet, if we could just suspend judgment a little longer, we might learn a little more. We could read other articles describing the Congressperson's actions in a different light. Maybe he's not such an idiot. Maybe we are missing some details on national events. But once we judge him, we won't dig into the events any further. We've already decided he's an idiot and that's it. Making matters worse, from this time forward, we will only be interested in information that feeds our viewpoint. This is because we tend to filter out competing perspectives to avoid the discomfort of challenge. It's called "confirmation bias."

In our judgment, we expose the limitations of our knowledge and run smack into our ignorance—the very ignorance we assigned to those we judged. We stop learning, we call everybody else "idiots," and in time, we become the idiot. Yes, *we become the idiot.*

Judge not, lest you….be judged.

JUDGING OURSELVES

A spiritual person judges all things.

True judgment begins with ourselves. Before we can wisely judge another person or situation, we must ask: To what extent am I…

- reacting?
- listening?
- seeking truth?
- a wise judge?
- willing to be wrong?
- open to information?
- tolerating ambiguity?
- suspending judgment?

Judgment gives us a handle by which to manage complex situations. It is much easier to call a politician a dolt than to admit that we don't know anything about the treaty governing the border of Canada and Montana, let alone the tax implications of removing tariffs on Moosehead beer in exchange for truckloads of Miller Lite. (Oh, those poor Canucks!)

We live in a complex world and much is demanded of us. Because I cannot act until I reach judgment, I am constantly called upon to make up my mind and take action on complex, gray-area issues. Often, what drives my judgmental tendencies is the innate need to gain a sense of mastery over my world.

The greater my tolerance of ambiguity, however, the better my judgments will be when it comes time to judge.

Which can be often. Let's face it: *A spiritual person judges all things.* Without judgment, we would have no standards, no ethics, no laws. We'd all be like tie-dyed hippies in a commune, sharing everything in common until someone takes too many of the organic beans. Then we bash them in the head.

The issue is life itself, and the question before the court, is how we wish to live: with an open mind or a closed mind?

Suspend judgment and open your life.

Judge everything and close your life.

Others will sense where you are in this spectrum and respond accordingly. Not unremarkably, relationship grows where judgment is suspended. And relationship is how we determine God's existence.

5

What Do We Mean by "God"?

DEFINITIONS DRIVE ANY ARGUMENT, any perspective. At heart, we are nearly all the same. Often, what divides us is not the issue but our perspective of the issue. At our cores, we are closer to one another than we think we are.

Consider the issue of abortion, a raging controversy in our modern times. It decides elections and drives extremists on both sides of the argument to commit heinous acts in the name of "truth." Abortion clinics are firebombed. Supreme Court justices are assailed. Politicians, desperate for votes, change sides repeatedly as public opinion vacillates in the shifting tides of warring influences.

The tools of this public battle, however, are definitions. Opponents of abortion use the term *child* to describe what is in a mother's womb, while proponents use *fetus*.

The difference is crucial.

In our hearts, none but the most depraved among us would willingly sanction the murder of children. You will not find anyone signing up for that position on any side of the issue. But a fetus is, by definition, non-human, whereas a child is a sentient human being.

For one side, abortion is the evacuation of unwanted tissue from a woman's body. For the other side, it's the killing of human life. The definitions enable each side to support their viewpoint.

The battle for the hearts and minds of society is being waged with vocabulary. As political sides stake their claims to the right of public opinion on any subject, a careful examination of tactics employed reveals the strategic use of language—again, *definition*. The talking points shot out of media cannons are designed to stake a claim to defining any event.

Consider, is it:

- a tax or a theft?
- a cow or a burger?
- a revolution or a rebellion?
- a murder or an assassination?
- an insurgent or freedom fighter?
- a dictator or a people's champion?
- a right to bear arms or an excuse for mass killers?

The battle for truth is waged through perceptions, and perceptions are driven by definitions—the definitions we accept and reject.

Now...which definitions do you accept and which do you reject...about God?

OUR DEFINITIONS OF GOD

Most of us have a definition of God, regardless of whether we accept or reject his existence. People who accept God's existence can, with a little prompting, describe in at least general terms the God they envision. Likewise, with a bit more prompting, those who reject God's existence can be specific about some of the characteristics of the God they are rejecting.

A friend of mine puts it like this: "No, Jim. I don't believe in the Mac Daddy in the sky."

> Mac Daddy / mac-da-dē / noun: "the all-encompassing provider, abundant giver of gifts, freely supporting, residing somewhere in the stratosphere."

Nearly every person in existence has encountered the concept of God in some form or fashion. This usually comes at an early age and may evolve throughout our lifetimes. Children seem most open to the idea of God. Perhaps having parents in close proximity makes the idea of an authoritarian provider hovering above them from the heavens more acceptable.

As we age, our definition of God evolves with our needs and experience. A small child's needs are simple: food, shelter and a blanket. As we reach out later in life, however, our needs evolve and the answers we crave become more complex: validation, security, fulfillment, achievement, purpose and accomplishment. Finally, we get old and find ourselves settling for what sustained long ago: food, shelter and a blanket.

Until challenged, most of us will never examine our definitions of God nor our needs that drive those definitions. To us, God is an absolute. It's like defining gravity or time or Monday night football. *It just is, OK?*

Saying *God* is like saying *sky*. What do we mean by sky? Do we mean…

- the blue dome above us?
- the place where clouds dwell?
- the air we breathe?
- the place where our dreams go?
- the composite of nitrogen, oxygen, water vapor, argon and carbon dioxide?

Just as it is important to look past the surface of human interactions, it is essential that we understand how we are defining God. Until we can define our terms, especially those in common usage, our communication is fruitless.

GENERAL IMPRESSIONS

While our definitions of God are intensely personal, some generalities will emerge as the sample set increases. Here are some common attributes which most people apply to God. They don't necessarily agree—some are outright opposing—but each side has enough representation to deserve mention.

God is: *Kind, just, loving, forgiving, healing, fair, meek, humble, loves the little children of the world.*

God is: *Judging, vengeful, angry, hateful, murderous, a terrible swift sword.*

God is: *Creator, provider, protector, guider, leader.*

God is: *Controller of everything*

God is: *Jealous, capricious, elusive, ambivalent.*

God is: *Aloof, separate, selective, separate, holier than thou.*

God is: *Male, female, non-human, super-human, light, spiritual, ethereal, timeless.*

God is: *Alive.*

God is: *Dead.*

Putting these all together, we have quite a selection:

- God is good.
- God is a judge.
- God is powerful.
- God is "up there."
- God lives in heaven.
- God looks out for us.
- God loves us remotely.
- God controls everything in life.
- God really doesn't care anymore.
- God took the last train for the coast.
- God is coming back to earth to rescue the faithful.
- God doesn't want to be involved with our daily lives.

Now, remember our earlier discussion. *What* we think is not nearly as important as *why* we think it. Our definitions of God come from somewhere. Understanding their origins helps us decide their usefulness in determining God's existence. Make no mistake, however—all definitions have value. They lead us in accepting God's existence or rejecting it.

Either way, our definitions of God reveal more about ourselves than about God.

All definitions of God have value.

All definitions are about us.

Let's see where our definitions come from.

6

Our Definitions of God

PEOPLE FORM RELATIONSHIPS according to their needs. Like covalent bonds among molecules, our needs drive us to join with others—our deficiency with their supply, our strength with their weakness. The nature of our fellow humans makes joining possible.

Consider marriage, one of the most intense relationships a person can experience. We marry for various reasons. It can be the need for intimate companionship, a secure relationship, a desire for children and a secure environment to nurture them. Or maybe we're just tired of sitting at home on Saturday night.

Notice that these reasons reflect deep needs; ones that cannot be met without another person.

The movie *Rocky* (1976) was about an amateur fighter rising from the streets of Philadelphia. The subtext, however, was his love for Adrian, the sister of his friend Paulie. Here's how Rocky explains it to her over-protective brother.

Paulie: [talking about his sister Adrian] You like her?

Rocky: Sure, I like her.

Paulie: What's the attraction?

Rocky: I dunno… she fills gaps.

Paulie: What's "gaps"?

Rocky: I dunno. She's got gaps, I got gaps. Together we fill gaps.

Ever notice that intimacy works best when another person is involved? And even though we believe child-rearing "takes a village," what is a village anyway? It's people...*other* people.

We form similar bonds in varying degrees of intimacy and commitment when we make friends, when we form working relationships, when we develop acquaintances with the people who cross our path. We have needs, and we naturally seek out relationships that meet those needs.

I'm dull, but I like people who are lively.

I'm quiet, so I like people who draw me out.

I'm hungry, which is why I enjoy people who can cook.

I think abstractly, so I pursue the company of logical people.

I'm independent, therefore I married a woman who grants me freedom.

Can it be any different in seeking a being we call *God*? If we bond with others based on our needs, is it possible that we also seek God based on our needs?

Consider our needs:

- our hunger
- our emptiness
- our loneliness
- our dreams
- our aspirations
- our hopes
- our joys
- our curiosity
- our questions
- our demands
- our wounds
- our weaknesses
- our fears
- our strengths
- our confidence
- our self-esteem

Needs. Gaps. Covalent bonds. Our lack and others' supply. It's how we bond as humans. Could it also be how we bond with God? Is this how he becomes real to us?

DESPERATION

The experience of having our needs met by someone or something makes that entity real. Indeed, the more intense the need, the more the thing which meets our needs becomes real.

Consider this simple logic:

We hunger and desire bread.

We thirst and desire water.

Does bread exist?

Yes.

Water?

Certainly. It has to exist.

Why? Why do these things have to exist?

Because we would die without them.

So, bread and water exist because they have to. The evidence of their existence is the fact that they sustain *our* existence.

Now let's take this a step further. Consider the statements:

I was starving and you gave me bread.

I was thirsty and you gave me water.

Therefore, I believe in you because you met my vital needs. You are bread and water to me.

That which met my basic needs became real to me.

What of other needs?

We fear and desire security.

We are lonely and desire love.

We fail and desire mercy.

We exist and desire purpose.

Is security a need? Certainly. Man can't live in uncertainty forever.

Is mercy a need? Yes. Everyone fails at some point. Mercy erases the negative effects of failure.

How about a sense of identity, purpose or fulfillment? Are these needs? They are. Do these needs get met? Sometimes they do, other times not, most times somewhere in between.

The higher we reach, the deeper the need. Like Maslov's triangle, we start with our basic needs and work our way up to the less tangible but equally vital needs. Eventually, we reach needs that we can't meet on our own. We need the help of something beyond ourselves. Sometimes these are needs at the bread and water level. Other times they are higher. Regardless of where they are, however, our needs will reach a point where only something beyond us can meet them.

We call that level *desperation*, a need beyond our ability, the point at which we reach up.

THE FINGER OF GOD

From the bible, there is the story of a reluctant deliverer named Moses whose God-given task was to confront Pharaoh of Egypt, the most powerful leader in the known world, and demand that he release his vast population of Jewish slaves for "three days of fun and music, and nothing but fun and music, and I God-bless you for it!" (Something like that.)

Of course, nothing in a good story ever goes according to plan, and this one is no exception. Pharaoh refused to release the Jews, which was quite understandable since the Jews were the backbone of the Egyptian economy. Yet Moses had a few aces up his sleeve. God had given Moses the power to do miracles—a show of force before Pharaoh and all of Egypt, the power of said God.

The first miracle was simple and profound. Standing before a defiant Pharaoh and his court of sycophants, Moses threw down his staff—he was a shepherd in his former life—and it turned into a snake. While the rest of the court was gasping, however, the cadre of magicians who surrounded Pharaoh all threw down their staffs and these also turned into snakes.

Moses 1. Magicians 21.

Not looking good for the visiting team. Here's the cool thing, though. Moses' snake? It ate the other snakes. Huuahh!

Still, Pharaoh remained undeterred. Those slaves weren't going anywhere, snakes or no snakes. So, Moses— never one to miss a great exit—blew out of the court with a threat. "You'll be sorry," he cried, or words to that effect.

A few days later, Moses called Pharaoh to the banks of the river Nile, touched the water with his staff (which presumedly had turned back into a stick by now, though a much fatter stick) and the Nile River turned into blood. This killed the fish and made the water undrinkable.

Remarkably, the Egyptian magicians did the same with their new staffs, and Pharaoh walked away muttering "Magic tricks. Psssht!"

A week later, an undeterred Moses made frogs appear and overrun the country, but the magicians duplicated this miracle as well. This amounted to a lot of frogs. (Pity it didn't happen in France.) Pharaoh, knee-deep in green slime and fearing he and his people were about to croak, begged Moses to call off his plague with the promise to let the Jews go on their sabbatical. So, Moses agreed and the frogs experienced a massive die-off.

After the mounds of frog corpses were piled up and hauled away, however, Pharaoh changed his mind and refused to free the slaves even for a few days.

Things were now getting tight. It was time to up the ante.

So Moses brought up lice and gnats in great clouds that looked like dust. They drove the people and their animals crazy. Here's the interesting thing, however. When the magicians, who had thus far replicated the snakes, blood-water and frogs, tried to conjure up lice and gnats, they failed.

They failed big time.

Now, failure is not remarkable, in and of itself. What makes this a cool story is what the magicians said to Pharaoh after failing.

Ready? They said they could not replicate the miracle because:

"This is the finger of God."

Of course, the rest is history...or, if you like, legend. After a few more plagues and promises and a lot of dead Egyptians, Pharaoh finally let the people go and the nation of Israel was born.

Now, what happened here? Pharaoh, along with all his court, could ignore God as long as they could keep up, miracle to miracle, with Moses. What did Pharaoh need this Hebrew God for? He could make his own blood river and frogs and snakes. Release the Jews? Screw that!

But then he reached a point where...he couldn't. He found himself staring into a void against the backdrop of utter failure. He must have felt alone—truly isolated—possibly for the first time in his life. He was desperate, willing to bargain.

I imagine Pharaoh would have related to Bob Dylan's lyrics right about then.

> *You say you never compromise*
> *With the mystery tramp, but now you realize*
> *He's not selling any alibis*
> *As you stare into the vacuum of his eyes*
> *And say do you want to make a deal?*

Bob Dylan

"So, Moses. How long did you say you'd be gone?"

SEEKING GOD

When people define God, they are often trying to make sense of their lives and the world around them. They are seeking something they cannot find elsewhere, so they define God in terms of what they think they need. Their resistance to the idea of God, however, is a factor in the pressure they feel as they reach out beyond themselves for answers. They are usually desperate. And this can involve key events and pain. Beneath every question, however, is an underlying assumption that forms the question and so drives the answer, especially our assumptions about God.

Here are some common assumptions:

Why did the earthquake happen?
    God willed it.

Why did the baby die?
    God wanted another little angel.

Why did I wreck my car?
    God is teaching you a lesson.

Why am I so confused?
    God is a mystery.

Notice the underlying definitions of God at the core of the answers to these tragic events:

God willed it.
    God's will determines what happens to us.

God wanted another little angel.
    God directs the taking of life.

God is teaching you a lesson.
    God uses calamity to make his points.

God is a mystery.
    God is beyond man and can't be understood.

Now, I am *not* arguing the accuracy of these definitions. I'm merely identifying our need-driven thought process when it comes to defining God. Our attempts to explain what happens to us, good or bad, reveal our underlying concepts of God.

In the end, we may decide that God didn't bring the earthquake; it just happened, a geological event inherent in the way the earth was created. We can also conclude that God doesn't kill babies because he's lonely or that he doesn't wreck cars to make a point. The key here is the process. This is typically how we form our concepts of God. What we do from there—accept or reject these concepts—is a part of who we are.

Reduced by pain to our most fundamental level, ascribing to God reasons for our pain means there is a God to blame. Likewise, praising God when things go well means there is a God to praise. And rejecting God means...there is a God to reject.

At least according to our definitions.

EXPECTATIONS

Our expectations drive us toward, or away from, the idea of God's existence.

Remember our earlier example: "I can't believe in a God who..."? Well, that reasoning operates in the lives of believers as well as non-believers.

The believer decides God can meet their needs; therefore, God exists.

The unbeliever decides that God can't meet their needs; therefore, God can't exist.

The difference is in how a person handles the choice to believe in God's existence.

The believer wants to believe and so forms a definition of God that works to accept God's existence.

The unbeliever doesn't want to believe and so forms a definition that works to deny God's existence.

If a person wants to believe in God, they define him in believable terms. If they don't want to believe in God, they define him in unbelievable terms.

The experience of God comes through the meeting of our needs. We understand this when we are willing to be open about our needs and how we think they are met.

NEEDS VS. EXISTENCE

There is another category of believer vs. unbeliever. The person who thinks *she needs nothing, therefore she doesn't need God*, slides easily but illogically into the camp of those who do not accept God's existence. Think about it. It's one thing to say "I don't need something." It's entirely different to say that a thing does not exist.

Of course, we are talking about a belief structure based on God meeting our needs. Still, the reasoning appears incongruous, does it not? The existence of something has nothing to do with our need for it. These are unrelated except, as I have been arguing, in determining our needs, perceptions and, by extension, what we accept as evidence.

Make no mistake about it. The existence of God does not rely on our acceptance of him. This is not Tinkerbell slowly dying because children no longer believe in fairies. Rather, this is people operating under faulty logic.

If you decide that God does not exist, own it. Live it. And be honest with yourself. Saying something cannot exist means there is no evidence of its existence—not that we have no need of it, but that there is no evidence of it...at least none we will accept.

Understanding what God offers, at least from a Christian perspective, sets the stage for accepting or rejecting God as he is revealed through the Christian experience.

The difference in human belief structures is the desire to believe or not believe. What drives this? What makes one person want to believe there is a God and another want to believe there is no God?

What is behind our behaviors? What drives us?

Let's consider this in the coming chapters.

7

Driven by Definition

WE CHOOSE WHETHER or not to believe in God's existence. But really, we are driven to our choices. Our definition of God either drives us to him or away from him. We run *from* a God we don't want and run *to* a God we do want.

Interestingly, the distinctions are not always between rejecting a harsh God or embracing a comforting God. People's choices can be surprising.

People who feel guilty, for example, carry a sense of deserved punishment. Definitions that will draw them to consider God's existence might be a God of mercy and forgiveness. Or they might seek a God of judgment and punishment as a means of appeasing the inner conflict between what they think is right and wrong with their conduct.

Likewise, a remote God, or no God at all, serves us well when we don't want a closer inspection of our lives. A relational God serves our needs for companionship when no one returns our calls or emails.

AS WE ARE

As we search for evidence of God's existence, we should look at our core needs first because they drive our definitions and affect how we interpret the evidence we find, for or against our viewpoint. To that end, we should consider:

What do we dream of?

What are we hungry for?

What does our life cry out for?

What do we desire in our deep heart's core?

What inadequacies do we rage against as we struggle to fulfill our visions?

Does it seem that everything around us—all that we have brought into life to fulfill the fundamental drive for purpose—only serves to sharpen our appetite for that which we can neither define nor live without?

> *There's a feeling I get*
> *when I look to the west*
> *and my spirit is crying for leaving.*

Robert Plant

We tend to define God by what we need and what we experience. As such, the evidence we ascribe to God's existence or non-existence says more about who we are than who God is.

> *We don't see things as they are.*
> *We see things as we are.*

Anis Nin

54

We are drawn to what we think will meet our needs. We seek what we think will satisfies us. The greater the need, the more intense the seeking. If we want something desperately and it meets our needs, it becomes real to us.

If I'm starving and someone gives me bread, that substance becomes real to me.

If I'm lonely and someone befriends me, they become real to me.

I believe in bread; the evidence of its existence is in the experience of it meeting my need for nourishment. I also believe in my friend. The intangible quality of friendship becomes real when it meets my need for companionship.

So, what do you need? And what are you willing to consider to meet those needs?

PURPOSE

One of our greatest needs is purpose—the answer to the questions: What am I here for? What am I supposed to do?

As long as we are meeting other people's immediate needs, however, we don't have to look much further for our purpose. A nursing mother, a school teacher, a sports team vying for a championship, soldiers in war—when we are vitally needed, we experience fulfillment. We have purpose.

Some people spend an entire lifetime wondering if they made a difference in this world. Marines don't have that problem.

Ronald Reagan

It's when the needs recede, however, that we become aware of a deeper need within ourselves—to find that unique contribution to life that only we can make. It's when the babies grow up, when our last class graduates, when we play the final game, when we ship back home to the arms of our loved ones and find ourselves spending every unguarded moment aching for our comrades in arms. It's when we reach the limit of our existence, sensing that whatever can truly fulfill us exists beyond ourselves in a realm we cannot name nor define. It's a place of its own choosing, where the rules we learned no longer apply. We hunger for what we do not know.

A sense of wondering about God may creep into our beings, perhaps an awareness we've suppressed or excused or rationalized away by saying we were doing good things in life. And in fact, we probably were. Most people do good things throughout their lives. Yet the deeper question is not one of good or evil, although we all have that struggle, but one of knowing, of awareness, of sensing our place in the greater universe and going after it with all our beings. In a word: *alive!*

Perhaps we are driven by the nagging sensation that there is more. We've followed the dictates of love. We've cared for our children and protected our comrades and stretched our capabilities with all the power within us. It is now time to look beyond ourselves for more than we are.

We have run with men and fought lions. It's time to fly with eagles.

A CREATOR

A definition of God that includes the creator of the universe serves us well in grasping our greater role in it. On the other hand, if there is no one and nothing above us, as John Lennon opined, then we can easily become a people most disillusioned. God as creator, of ourselves and all we see around us, places us somewhere in relationship to him like a parent to their children. Seeing ourselves as part of the creation of God implies a new identity. What was once the limit of our being now becomes the foundation of our purpose, propelling us into an infinite realm we've only dreamed of in our greyscale musings.

Can God be defined like that? Could it really be so simple? If there is a creation, is there a creator? If there is love, is there a source of love? Could that be it?

Can we reach out to that source, through the void that challenges all we've known, to find limitless meaning to a seemingly limited life? Do we dare risk it?

The first step is facing the void.

The second step is not turning away.

We call these steps *faith*.

8

Faith and Reason

LEAP FROGGY LEAP

ANY DISCUSSION OF GOD'S existence has to consider the concept of faith. In the lexicon of popular opinion, it is widely held that the belief in anything undetectable to the five senses requires a decision to believe in it—a decision that defies tangible evidence or intelligent reason. This belief is often referred to as a *leap of faith*, or a *blind leap of faith*.

Such a leap is understood as being an act of the will regardless of the facts, the determination to accept the existence of something despite the lack of supporting evidence. As such, faith is often considered anti-intellectual, something done out of emotion, the sustenance of the weak or desperate. In a word: *foolish*.

As with the concept of God, this popular definition of faith has little to do with actual faith and everything to do with ourselves. Indeed, such a definition only serves to support our preconceived notions—our reasons to either believe in God or not believe. People who hold to a fuzzy concept of God will reach for him in undefined ways, and

59

those who distance themselves from God will do so in favor of what they consider the antithesis of faith in God: evidence.

Tragically, these concepts are not descriptions of faith.

Faith, as understood by those who actually practice it, is not belief without evidence. In fact, it is just the opposite. Faith is belief *with* evidence. A working synonym for faith could be *experience*.

Let's look closer at this idea.

Faith is a belief structure supported by experience. It leads one to expect an outcome based on previous outcomes.

For example, have faith that my truck will start. If I get in and turn the key, I expect it to start. Why? Because I read in the manual that it's a great truck? No. Because it's started for the past 1,000 times.

Now, can I guarantee it will start every time? Of course not. It could blow a circuit or suck in some bad gas and I'd be sitting and fuming. But it's done so well for so long that I don't even think about it. I have faith in the truck's starting ability.

There was a time, however, when I wasn't so confident of my vehicles' reliability. That was when I bought cars for a few hundred dollars and didn't even ask if they ran. It didn't matter. For a few bucks, I'd make it run. Yet I never left the house without a toolbox in the back seat.

I once rebuilt a '72 Corolla with a few hundred thousand miles on it. I bought it from an ex-nun I was dating. The relationship didn't last (she had a few bad habits) but the car was a keeper. It needed a valve job, a head gasket, new hoses and belts, and the removal of a squirrel nest in the trunk. I finished the work with a high degree of confidence, but the first time I turned the key, I wasn't sure it would start. I knew I'd done a good job, and I desperately needed a car, so I certainly hoped it would start. Yet I didn't know what it would do until I heard the starter engage and the engine cough to life.

My faith on that first try was small, but there was some faith. I knew it was a good car and that I was a good mechanic, so there was a reasonable chance that it would fire up after the overhaul. But certain? No. Faith? Yes. Based on what? Based on evidence: good car, good mechanic, good God please start!

After that first time, my faith in the car's reliability grew. In the beginning, I only took it out for a few blocks for fear that something would break down. But gradually, I expanded the territory of trust to include many hundreds of miles. The car never let me down, and my faith in it grew accordingly.

Keep in mind that every new trip I took extended the boundaries of my faith. At one point, I knew the car would go 100 miles because it had often done so. But could it go 200 miles? It took the extension of my faith to try, but it was worth the risk.

So, what made my faith grow? Small steps, small risk, favorable results. With every measured risk, I extended my faith into the unknown, to regions where I did not have evidence of the car's reliability. Would we call this a leap of faith? The opposite of reason? Acting on an utter lack of any discernable evidence?

Of course not.

Why, then, do people say that a belief in God requires a leap of faith, abandoning all reason and going for an emotional connection with an invisible, unprovable being? Perhaps the reason is that they've never been around the block with this being. Perhaps they've never trusted God— or the concept of God—for anything, so faith in God's existence might as well be a flying leap at the moon as far as they're concerned. Or maybe they did trust God in something, and that thing didn't come to pass; the child died, the bank foreclosed, the cancer spread, or the father left home. For them, the existence of God is a far distant concept lacking credibility.

NICE CATCH

When I was a boy of eight years old, I was searching for my baseball mitt. I knew I'd left it somewhere in the backyard, but I couldn't find it. Frustrated, I remember what the men in my Sunday School class had told us about God and prayer—that he answers it. Religious training wasn't big in our household. Mom was a single mother battling alcoholism and I was left to run the streets of a small town in Pennsylvania. It was a great childhood if you don't count parental involvement. (Something I rarely did.) On Sunday mornings while mom slept in, I'd load up my brother and we'd ride our bicycles across town to the local church for Sunday school. It was taught by large men more comfortable with tractors and cornfields than theology. Yet there was something in their humble faith that reached my heart.

On that morning in the backyard, with mom nursing a hangover and little league waiting for me, I resolved to follow the example of the believing farmers. "God, where is my baseball mitt?"

Immediately, a picture formed in my mind. It was my mitt lying on the floor of my treehouse. With a skip and a bound, I was up that tree and cheering. There was my mitt just as I saw it in my mind's eye.

A small step, but one I never forgot as I build upon it.

Fifteen years later found me in Navy electrician school. I'd been away from my wife and kids for four months and I was at the end of my rope. It was late at night. I leaned my head against the cold panes radiating the stark reality of a north Chicago winter. Freezing rain pelted the glass as my heart shuddered. One by one, I released my pain to God, recounting for him (in case he wasn't paying attention) how I'd left my family to join the Navy, and now that boot camp and tech school were about over, I realized that my separations were just beginning. Apparently, the Navy has these things called *ships*. And ships, last I checked, spend time at sea. A lot of time. It was more than I had the heart for, given the precarious situation of my marriage and fledgling fatherhood. I knew my domestic scene would crater if I was absent much longer.

My final prayer of the night was as simple as a boy looking for a baseball mitt. "God, are you there? Because it feels like you aren't. I keep dialing your number but you aren't answering."

More of a plea than a complaint. Reality sucks at times, but it's a requisite starting point.

The next morning, I sat in class and surveyed my classmates. We'd been getting our orders sporadically for the past three weeks. Mine hadn't come yet, but others were cheering or bemoaning theirs.

"Hey, I got a destroyer."

"I got sub school! Yes!"

"I'm gonna be a plank owner on the Nimitz!"

"Oh crap, I'm on a tender."

Me... I got nothing. Nothing but dread.

Then around 10 am, the Chief of the school stuck his head in the door to trumpet these fateful words: "You got a Fireman Bryson in here?"

"Yessir, Chief," I responded.

"Get out here," he barked.

I was a dead man walking. I didn't know what I'd done, but it was over, whatever "it" was.

In the hall, his tone shifted into high gear. (I'll edit for those unfamiliar with Navy vocabulary.)

"Bryson, who the @#$%&^ do you know?"

"Sir?"

"The Chief of Naval Operations' office just called. They need an electrician for his personal yacht." (Navy term: *barge*.)

"Sir, what does that have to do with—?"

"They asked for YOU!"

"Huh?"

"@#$#@#@%$ Bryson, do you want the assignment or not?"

"Um...sir...is that shore duty?"

"Oh for &^%@#$!! Yes, Bryson, that's shore duty. Washington DC. You want it? 'Cause they asked for you or another guy. But they wanted you first."

A hundred thoughts raced through my mind in that instant, but only one word escaped."

"YesSirIwanttheassignmentSir."

I'd gone from laying my soul bare before God the night before, to the staff of the Navy's top Admiral calling my name for the best duty in the Navy. Think that built my faith? Um...yeah, it did.

Trust is formed in steps. We learn to trust something on a small scale at first. This is faith in its infancy. As trust grows, so does our willingness to risk further. If the girlfriend still likes us after six months, perhaps we will buy an engagement ring. If the medicine relieves our symptoms, perhaps we will heal. We grow in faith as we learn to trust.

When doctors want to lengthen a bone to extend a leg damaged by injury or deformity, they position the upper and lower bone pieces about a quarter-inch apart. The idea is that the bones will grow toward each other, and as they do, the doctors move the bones a little farther part, repeating the process over a span of months until the bone is the right length and strength.

Faith in God—one of reliance, adherence and allegiance—grows the same way. As we willingly extend our faith, we see results that either cause us to want to go further or retreat to a lower level. This is not a leap of faith, but the cultivation of faith in measured steps based on reason. If it is reasonable to trust a truck to start or a friend to answer a call or the police to respond to 911, is it not also reasonable to have faith in God as revealed through our needs and definitions?

Remember our predilections, however. A person with little inclination to discover God will decry the "leap of faith" as an unacceptable requirement to believe in God. On the other hand, the person desperate for something beyond themselves will extend their heart to a spiritual entity they can neither define nor fully relate to. And while it would be easy to deride this action as another "leap of faith," let us consider that those who have lost everything are often willing to try anything. The fact that something seems to answer drowning people who climb aboard a boat without asking where that boat is headed, speaks to the forbearance of whatever receives them.

LIVE BY FAITH?

Funny how rational people claim to eschew faith in their daily lives. But considering how they view faith—that it is the opposite of reason—their position is understandable. Who wants to be foolish? Only a fool. Assuming a more accurate definition of faith, however—one that involves the basis of experience—it becomes clear that every rational person lives by faith.

Take tap water, for example. I turn the spout, fill the glass and drink, believing that it will satisfy my thirst. But how do I know? The water could be poison. It could contain a deadly virus. Did I analyze the water? Give it to the dog first? Test it on prisoners? Of course not. Why not? Because I've drank from that tap every day for years. It's never hurt me and it never will.

Now...think about what I just said:

"It's never hurt me (*fact*) and it never will (*faith*)."

It's a fact that it hasn't hurt me yet (as far as I know). But can I guarantee that it won't ever hurt me? No. But I live as if it is entirely safe. I live...based on experience...based on faith.

STEERAGE

Understanding how faith works, the next question is easy: Faith...in what?

We are driven by what we believe. I believe something will bring me happiness so I gravitate toward it like it's free money. I believe something will bring me sorrow so I avoid it like the plague. Want to know what steers a person? What sets their course? It's faith. We draw toward what we want, believing it will be there, and steer away from what we don't want, believing it will hurt us.

Faith, then, is very real to all of us. My life, your life, everybody's lives, are determined in large part by what we are willing to believe—our faith. And that is reinforced by what we experience.

Is it possible that faith in something called God could come a little at a time as we try to trust this God? In the beginning, people are driven to God by their needs. Then, as their needs are met, their trust in this being grows. Gradually, we begin to understand what it is into which we have put our fledgling faith.

The God of the bible is vast. He is presented in ways that stretch our imagination and easily outstrip our present experiences. It is only when we step out and believe in areas that are beyond us that we grow past our present circumstances. Still, it is not a *leap* into the unknown, but rather measured steps, understanding what we are betting on even if we don't yet see it all.

In the final analysis, saying there cannot be a God because belief requires a leap of faith, starts to sound like a cheap excuse, one more reason to hold back in fear, pride, pain or ego. There are a hundred reasons why people do not approach the concept of God in ways that could prove or disprove his existence. The mischaracterization of faith as a leap into foolishness is a rationalization that drives people to take a leap of their own—that of ignoring a preponderance of evidence both within and without them.

9

What Evidence?

Yes, the search for God's existence is deeply personal, but that doesn't mean we have to go it alone.

What if something exists but I don't know it because I cannot perceive it? Remember, we are the means by which we experience all that is around us—our senses, our thoughts and feelings, our observations and experiences. Yet we are all different. So, is it possible that no two of us—unique creatures that we are—will experience the same thing the same way?

The wind blows, leaves rustle, a flag flutters, a shutter bangs, a cow turns away, a mother zips her jacket, a farmer studies the clouds and a child races for her kite.

Does the wind exist? Well, look at the leaves, the flag, the shutter, the cow, the mom, the kite. Something is moving them. One wind; different reactions. But if all we see is the effect, we miss the source. Does the wind exist or not? Well, what will we accept as evidence?

The logic is simple. If God exists, there should be evidence. If God does not exist, there should be no evidence. Think about the burden of proof in such a scenario, however. Because it is impossible to prove a negative, no proof is required, nor any evidence other than the utter lack of evidence to support God's existence. So...even *one shred of evidence* supporting God's existence negates the evidence-less assertion that God does not exist. It only takes one candle...

The question of God's existence now turns. What will we accept as evidence? What single photon of light, admitted by our credibility filters, will shatter the darkened visage of a godless world?

As we have said, the evaluation of evidence of God's existence is deeply personal, driven by our definitions of God which are influenced by our needs. Indeed, this is how it has to be. We are the instruments measuring this world and all that is in it, and we are unique beings.

But what else can influence us? What of the experiences of others? Perhaps those who came before us? Even those who have come after us and have gone back in time to leave us clues? (OK, that's a stretch. We'll leave the future to better storytellers.)

Can we accept something without experiencing it firsthand? We might take someone's word for it. Or we might say "Show me!" Indeed, we do that a lot, don't we? We decide to take someone's word for something or we reject their word altogether. We do it all the time, and our lives depend on it.

I have never seen an atom, but I believe they exist because I believe the people who say they have observed atoms. These people are scientists, way smarter than I am, and they have letters after their names. Come to think of it, there are many things I believe exist even though I don't have firsthand knowledge of them.

I've never been to Antarctica, but I figure those penguins at the Bronx Zoo came from somewhere. I never met Mother Teresa, but I hear good things about her. Likewise for Alexander Graham Bell, Jonas Salk, Albert Einstein and Elvis...and I'm not sure about Elvis.

People have been writing about God for as long as there has been recorded history. Consider the major religions of the world. Could it be the same wind, just different experiences?

What will we accept as evidence?

THE ENCYCLOPEDIA

Two thousand years ago, people in the Middle East were writing about a new religion based on the life, death and resurrection of a person they claimed was the savior of the world. Gradually, and under various motives, a collection of 66 books by 40+ authors spanning 2,000 years was assembled into a common volume. This collection of books entailed history, poetry, songs, wisdom, law, prophecy and revelation. Since that time, it has been studied, debated, revered and challenged by the learned and unlearned. And while much debate continues, the core principles of the books remain constant:

1. There is a God.

2. This God is involved with mankind.

What will we accept as evidence?

Thousands of years ago, video recorders didn't exist. Of course, neither did penicillin. But here's the point. The writers of the books gave us their best evidence. They wrote things down as faithfully as they could, and those who compiled the books did not shy from controversy. Instead of one book on the life of this savior, for example, they provided four—and these books differed in significant places. Likewise, instead of one writer of the new theology, they offered several, along with a history of the early Christian church and its struggles. Certainly, some things were kept out of the compilation, but enough was included to demonstrate flawed people in relationship with something they call "God."

Interestingly, historians tell us that many of the people depicted in the stories died for what they believed. And that these deaths were hideous. Would people have endured torture and died for legends? Perhaps. But this continues today. People throughout the world base their lives on, and willingly die for, what they believe is the truth written in the collection of books we call the bible.

Although I am writing from a Christian perspective, if there is evidence of God's existence, we should be able to find it anywhere...even in Christianity.

People describe a wind and act accordingly. I don't see the wind but I see their response. Could this be God?

What will we accept as evidence?

If I am looking for evidence of God's existence, I have to be open to other people's experiences. I have to consider the possibility that others have perceived God in ways that have convinced them of his existence...even if I have not had the same experiences. I don't mean I have to accept what everyone has said and done, but my integrity requires me to consider a preponderance of evidence in the way of others' experiences, observations and perceptions.

Millions upon millions have responded to an urging in their hearts and come away saying they have experienced God in ways they hadn't imagined. Many of these people reorient their lives toward this God and serve him for the rest of their days. Why?

Remember—it only takes one shred of evidence to dispel the notion that God doesn't exist. Yet the search must be understood for what it is. Recall our definitions of God. We are really asking: *Does the God we envision exist?*

The God we envision is the God we define. Being real about our definitions allows us to investigate his presence in ways we have not yet considered, looking for a god we have not envisioned. It's the idea that perhaps God is different than we imagine, different even than the God we presently accept or reject.

To be clear, I am not advocating that God's existence is dependent on our ability to define him or even know him. A thing is what it is, regardless of how we define it or experience it.

> *"What's in a name? That which we call a rose*
> *By any other name would smell as sweet."*

William Shakespeare

Our knowledge of anything—God, the weather, motorcycles, good books, fine wine, roller derby, the vast blue ocean—merely affects our ability to experience it.

If I do not know what a motorcycle is, how likely am I to experience one? Lacking an appreciation of its existence, I am not likely to climb aboard and attempt to set the land speed record for two-wheeled locomotion in a tee-shirt and a brain bucket.

Believers in God express empirical evidence of his existence by saying he manifests in their lives. Notably, his presence often aligns with their expectations. If they expect God to bless them, for example, he seems to do just that. And if they expect God to curse them, they seem to receive the same from God. Their experience of God changes, however, as their expectations change.

Some say this is evidence of God being created by man through his expectations. However, another explanation exists, that this is evidence of our expectations filtering our experiences of God. If this is true that our expectations limit our experiences, then changing our expectations, indeed, reorienting expectations, will change our ability to perceive God.

Consider: The idea that God is love seems to open a floodgate of love into the heart of the believer. Many testify of just such an occurrence. Likewise, the idea that God is a provider seems to release such provision in people's lives. Again, what they believe about God seems to drive what they experience of God.

Of course, God, if he exists at all, is what he is. Our knowledge of God does not change who or what he is. But when our expectations change our perceptions, then it behooves us to compare those expectations against those of others, especially those who write passionately about their experiences of God.

Here is what people in the bible have written about the God they experience. At the very least, we should consider their viewpoints in our search.

Is God love? The Apostle John thought so.

Dear friends, let us love one another, for love comes from God. Everyone who loves has been born of God and knows God. Whoever does not love does not know God, because God is love.

Does God provide? The Apostle Paul thought so.

And my God will meet all your needs according to the riches of his glory in Christ Jesus.

Is God forgiving? Again, from the Apostle John.

If we confess our sins, he is faithful and just and will forgive us our sins and purify us from all unrighteousness.

Does God want to be a part of our lives?

Yet to all who did receive him, to those who believed in his name, he gave the right to become children of God— children born not of natural descent, nor of human decision or a husband's will, but born of God.

Can God be trusted? Balaam thought so.

God is not human that he should lie, not a human being that he should change his mind. Does he speak and then not act? Does he promise and not fulfill? I have received a command to bless; [God] has blessed, and I cannot change it.

Even if you lack the context of these writings, is it fair to say that the people who wrote these things were experiencing God in some way? Again, they didn't have modern technology. They could record video and post on YouTube. Writing was all they had.

These experiences continue to this day. A prominent preacher from California, Kris Vallotton, talks about hearing the audible voice of God as a teenager. Not a Christian yet, Kris asked God to heal his mother of a skin disease. God answered him audibly, and the next morning, his mother was healed.

Now, not everyone claims to hear an audible voice. Nor does everyone see instant responses to prayers. The fact that some people experience these things could be considered evidence of a God who bears a resemblance to what these people were writing about.

Remember, most of us have never seen an atom or walked through Antarctica, but we believe what we are told by those who do. I've never seen the Civil War, but I believe the history. I wasn't there when the liberty bell rang and Independence was declared for the 13 Colonies, but I live in the United States of America. I never shook Theodore Rosevelt's hand to thank him for creating our national park system, but I believe he created them. I walk through federal parks many times a year.

I have not experienced God the way Kris Vallotton did, but he says he did, and I have listened to Kris teach on many other subjects and found him to be a credible person.

It is impossible to prove everything that people claim to have experienced. We are not timeless nor unlimited in our comprehension. At some point, I have to accept what quantum physicists say about the universe, what doctors say about the treatment, what instant replay says about the touchdown.

We all live this way.

And at some point, I have to give credibility to the writings of the historians, the prophets and the artists of the bible...all witnesses to something greater than I have experienced in my life. If nothing else, I can use their lives to keep an open mind to what might be, the possibility that I don't know everything.

If there is one thing that life teaches me, it's that I don't know everything.

Maybe there's more about God than I can presently experience. Maybe I can use what others have found as an indication of where my blind spots are, where my ignorance begins and my lack of appreciation starts. Maybe I could learn something.

What will we accept as evidence?

If we believe God is just, and we find justice somewhere in the world, is that evidence of God's existence?

If we believe God is a provider, and we find provision somewhere in the world, is that evidence of God's existence?

If we believe God is love and we find love somewhere in the world, is that evidence of God's existence?

If justice and provision and love exist in places, even though they don't exist everywhere, where do they come from?

don't all agree! Shocking, isn't it? I mean, if something is true or not, shouldn't everyone agree on it? And yet there it is in plain sight—absolute chaos. As I approach the wooden rail, intent on making my choice, my friends are already arguing, staking out their positions. It's disheartening. Why can't we agree on this most fundamental aspect of life? Can't we all just get along?

I, as a potential convert to the idea, am perplexed when I see not one spout but hundreds, each beckoning for my attention. Do I want a stout? Or an IPA? A wheat? Or a pilsner? It's too much!

How can people say that beer exists when there are so many varieties of expression? I can't handle this. I'm shaken to the core. I flee the brewery in disillusionment. My friends were lying to me. It's all a hoax. Mind over matter. The power of suggestion. A blind leap of suds.

And yet...people dedicate their lives, not just to beer but to beer making! Monks in monasteries, hipsters in LA, middle-aged retirees moving to Montana for the mountain springs to brew their ale with the slogan "Good For What Ales Ye!"

At my lowest point, I'm hit with a revelation. Maybe beer is bigger than I thought. Maybe beer is not just to meet my needs, but the needs of others as well.

I shake my head. No way. Beer is beer. It never changes. How can I trust something that looks like one thing to one person and something completely different to another?

In panic, I flee in a dead run and make my way for the very thing I know will meet my innermost need. The door flies open and a smiling greeter ushers me inside. Fortunately, no beer in sight. Thankful that I've found meaning at last, I cry in lusty tones:

"I want a motorcycle!"

"Ah," says the greeter in tones reserved for a mortuary. "And which one would you like?"

"Which one?" I ask, incredulous. "You know, one with wheels, handlebar, a motor that goes Potato Potato Potato..."

The greeter stares. He waves his arm expansively. I look around. Motorcycles everywhere. But wait...they're all different. One bike, two bikes, red bikes, blue bikes! No!!! Big bikes, little bikes, tall bikes, short bikes, fast bikes, slow bikes.

I crawl out the same door that, moments earlier, ushered me into what I was positive would bring me peace.

My hopes dashed, my heart shattered, with nothing left to do but retch and die, I hear a faint sound carried on the breeze. It beckons my aching soul. It's a bell tolling for me, and it seems to be coming from yonder white tower.

Surely, I'll find peace there.

10

God or the Things of God?

THERE IS A DIFFERENCE between who God is and who we need him to be. The distinction is God's being vs. God's function. His being is objective: God is who he is, period. His function is subjective: my experience of God is based on what I perceive him to be.

Both perspectives are useful in uncovering his existence, but they are radically different in their approach.

Let's use human relationships first as an example, and then we'll see how this applies to God. We approach people in either capacity: being or function, depending on the situation.

If I stand before a judge, I expect fair judgment. I couldn't care less who the judge is. She could love cat videos and despise grumpy old men. She could listen to techno-pop music and dance the macarena at midnight. She could stand on grassy knolls and throw rocks at 747's. I couldn't care less as long as she judges my case fairly. It's her function that I care about.

Likewise, if I enter a tavern, I am looking for friendliness and refreshment. The bartender could even be a Dallas Cowboys fan! (Perish the thought!) But as long as he's good at pouring beer, we are gonna be best buds for as long as I'm warming a bar stool.

Now, consider who we marry. When a woman meets a prospective candidate for her hand in marriage, she might notice the things he does. If the candidate listens when she speaks, if he is thoughtful and considers her needs, if he grooms well and baths at least once a week (whether he needs it or not), he's probably passed the first review.

But more is coming, because the woman knows what a man rarely knows—that she's not marrying what he does but who he is. So, she will begin to look deeper. What he *does* can be conditioned, yet what he *is* cannot be changed...not really. She might get him to up the hygiene schedule by a few days, but if he sticks to his momma like a little boy, that behavior is probably there to stay. It's tied to who he is—insecure and desperate for maternal approval.

Why is this important to our search for God's existence? Because functions are not objective. They are subjective. They easily make God whatever we want him to be, and then we judge God based on false expectations.

LOST IN THE AMAZON

I love books. All kinds of books, old and new. One book, two books, red book, blue book. So, imagine my delight when I meet Fred at church (not his real name; of course it's not! I mean, who names their kid *Fred*?) and I discover that Fred works for Amazon. Yay! So, I immediately strike up a conversation.

"Hey, so what do you guys do with all those books that people return?"

"I dunno. Throw them out, I guess. Why?"

"Can I have them?"

"All of them?"

"Well, you know. Maybe just a truckload or two."

"A truckload?"

"You know. Now and again, holidays and weekends. Maybe Christmas, New Years, Valentine's Day, Arbor Day, Presidents Day, Administrative Professionals Day..."

"OK, Jim. I'll see what I can do."

And so the relationship proceeds. He calls me when they are tossing out books, and we grow to become fast friends.

But...are we?

There comes a day when he can't get any more books for me. That's when it hits me. What do I know about Fred? His family? His kids? His likes and dislikes? What moves him? Makes him cry or sing? What does he dream of or yearn for?

I don't know who Fred is. I only know what he can do for me. I don't know the man. And it's not because he is closed or guarded. It's because I'm not seeking him. I'm seeking what he can do for me. And because he is a good guy, he obliges me...for a while, perhaps thinking that a more meaningful relationship will emerge. But it never does. Entering a relationship expecting to change the other person rarely works as intended.

> *Love is not love*
> *Which alters when it alteration finds,*
> *Or bends with the remover to remove.*
> *O no! it is an ever-fixed mark*
> *That looks on tempests and is never shaken;*
> *It is the star to every wand'ring bark,*

William Shakespeare, Sonnet 116

When we approach the idea of God's existence, even the concept of God, we are typically motivated by our immediate needs and our perception of a God to meet those needs.

Let's be honest: When it comes to God, we are dealing in perceptions, impressions, hunger, want, lack, needs inexpressible, and the hope of satisfaction at levels we can barely articulate.

Of course, a benevolent God will meet us there if we let him. My young kids don't have to know me deeply for me to provide for them. Hey, you need diapers? I'll get you diapers. A tricycle? Not a problem. Apple iPhone 50? Forget it. I already have a second mortgage.

Later, in 60 years or so, we might have a talk about all I've learned in life and what I'd like in a nursing home. For now, however, I'm pleased to take care of them.

Yet a healthy relationship cannot remain solely at the needs level. Why "healthy"? Because basing our evidence of

God's existence on what he does rather than who he is, opens us to shifts in our perception of him based on our experiences—how we are doing at getting our needs met at the time.

I was in tight with Fred as long as I got books. But when the Dickens' and Steinbecks and Faulkners stopped flowing, the relationship tanked. Fred could have disappeared for all I cared, and he did to my perception.

Ultimately, the search for God's existence must move beyond our needs. We must eventually approach God on his terms. As we said, most definitions of God are about who we are, not who he is. Fundamentally, a thing is what it is. "A" is "A," as Ayn Rand famously declared. In this case, God either is or is not.

The variance comes in our perception of God's existence. If I have to decide, I must base it on objective evidence, not subjective need.

The fact that many claim to have experienced God through the meeting of their needs can be understood as evidence of his care for people who turn their hearts to him. For them—for all of us—that meeting of needs becomes the evidence for God's existence. Yet for others, especially those who have a pretty good handle on life and are looking for something deeper, that kind of evidence thins quickly. Why believe in God who helps me make my mortgage if my house is paid off? Perhaps he can help me manage my investments instead.

Some needs are immediate and material, while others are deep and eternal.

CHANGING GOD

Comedians are having a lot of fun these days with people in our society who "identify" as something other than what they appear to be. Just last month I read about a motorcyclist who identifies as a bicyclist and was breaking all the records at the Tour de France.

Now, lest I sound insensitive, some of these issues deserve careful attention. Nothing is funny about someone who is genuinely conflicted about their gender, their race or their place in the universe.

The underlying concept here is the issue of our identity aligning with our beliefs. *I am what I think I am, not what I appear to be.* Again, this is a gross generalization, but it serves a point.

As we approach the concept of God with our needs and desires, we have to accept that what we want God to be does not drive what he is.

Do you accept that?

It's like arguing with the IRS. You may identify as a lost planetary traveler on temporary hiatus from your deep space sojourn, but your gonna have to pay your taxes while you cool your jets here on Terra Firma.

When people conceive of God, they typically think of an all-powerful, all-knowing being who either is, or is not, involved in our lives. What they miss is that they can't see beyond their own desires. They ascribe qualities to that God based on their needs.

If there is a God, that God is who he is. He just *is*. And all our attempts to typify him serve only to highlight our inability to comprehend him further.

ROCK ON

There was a giant rock in the harbor sticking up 100 feet. The fishermen loved it. It was a great place to find oysters, crabs and schools of fish. The sailors hated it. It was always in the way. At night, it was difficult to see. More than a few ships had been ruined by misjudging the currents around the rock.

Whether people saw the rock as a provision or an obstruction, the rock was the rock. It didn't change with people's perspectives.

Likewise, God—if he exists—doesn't change with our conception of him. Only our perceptions change. We tend to define God as we experience him, and we rarely move past our expectations to define him further.

As such, we need something more. We need a standard. We need a record. We need the experiences of others to augment our experiences of God, to define him so that we can determine his existence—not our perception of his existence, but his actual existence.

There's this book...though it's not really a book. More like an encyclopedia of 66 books written by 40+ authors spanning thousands of years. And it's pretty interesting.

11

Truth and Fiction

SINCE IT'S OUR DEFINITIONS of God that frame our search for God's existence, can you see that false definitions of God—those that fail the reality test—can drive a person to believing God does not exist? If you are expecting something that can't possibly exist, or if you are trying to fit your definition into a concept that is unworkable or unhealthy, it will discredit your search and drive you to abandon it altogether.

Knowing this, some people like to throw obstacles in the way of those searching for God, indeed searching for something different and beyond the norm. No matter how progressive we think we are, seeing one of the flock stand up and declare "Wait! We don't all have to be sheep!" can be disconcerting. Nobody likes the status quo disrupted when they are, or want to be, the status quo.

As an impressionable teenager, my agnostic father challenged my assertion that God existed. He used a simple word trick to addle my thinking.

"Can God do anything?" he demanded.

"Yes," I said, full of youthful conviction.

"Can God make a rock?"

"Sure. He made all the rocks."

"Can God make a big rock?"

"Of course."

"Can God pick up that big rock?"

"Sure he can."

"Can God make a rock so big that he can't pick it up?"

"Well...yes, er...no. I guess so. I don't know!"

He had me there. God can't do everything...or can he? I gave up on my God-search for several months after that. During that time, I drifted into the company of a few friends who had different ideas for finding enlightenment, especially late at night.

See, we can make excuses. We can even create clever logic games. What we can't do is discover the truth about God's existence if we aren't seriously looking. If we don't care, we don't care. There will be plenty of reasons to validate our choices leading us elsewhere. It's easy. People do it all the time. The hard part is going against the flow—both the agnostic flow and the religious flow. Upon closer examination, these are one and the same.

GREEK DIVISION

Western society in particular seems vexed with ways of thinking about God that are flat-out contradictory. In all fairness, however, much of that thinking is rooted in Greek philosophy.

Plato was a Greek philosopher who lived somewhere around 400 BC (BC: Before Computers). He had a lot of good ideas interspersed with a few murky notions, but in the realm of God and spirituality, he had one big mistaken concept.

Plato thought a lot about God. Of course, he thought a lot about everything, but the subject of God and the "unseen" world particularly vexed him. He finally reasoned that if God existed, he must be so far above humans that he'd be impossible to relate to. Therefore, God must dwell elsewhere, apart from man. This led Plato to the concepts of a spiritual world and a natural world. Plato's spiritual world is where God exists, and the natural world is where humankind exists. He then imagined a separation between what we know as earth and where the angels gather for karaoke.

Such thinking led to the concept of a God being *up* in heaven, aloof and apart from man—those pitiful creatures staring up at the clouds and wondering where their next meal is coming from.

Can you see what Plato's concept of God does to the definition of God? Is this a portrait of a relational God; a God who speaks to the inner hearts of people, relating to their needs and seeking to meet those needs? Remember, it's our needs that lead us in our search for God.

This image of heaven above earth also discourages our search for evidence of something greater, something beyond our existence. How can we hope to find truth that is so far removed from our existence?

But what if Plato was wrong? What if the spirit realm and the natural realm are intertwined? You know that quiver you get just before the phone rings with traumatic news? Or when you look at your best friend and say what she was thinking? Or when you bet a hunch on a person and it is confirmed in spades? That's the spiritual side of us informing the natural side. How many times do we hear: "I'm spiritual but not religious"? What does it mean to be "spiritual"? Doesn't this, at a rudimentary level of definition, bring spirit together with natural? Like gas in a car, right?

What if God has been speaking to us on the inside to our hearts, but we have been preoccupied with staring up at the heavens like little birds waiting for the next worm to drop from the sky?

What if God has been speaking to us in tones of love, justice, provision and wisdom for so long that we eventually ascribe these qualities to ourselves, not considering that he might be the source of these things?

What if I have driven a Ford truck for so many years that the name *Ford* becomes a household term for sturdy transportation of goods and services? Meanwhile I forget (or never learn) about a man named Ford who built an assembly line in the early 20th century to bring affordable vehicles to an eager public?

What if God is all around us and we don't recognize him as such?

THE OMNIS

A lot of misinformation about God in our Western culture comes from people's interpretation of the bible. Keep in mind that anything written must be interpreted to make any sense. When people educated in the West read stories of a society of nomadic tribesmen in the Middle East, some things are bound to be misunderstood. It's gonna happen. There are thousands of years and vast oceans of culture between us. We can't wish ourselves into alignment with ancient historians, but we can educate ourselves so that our search for truth is an informed one.

An ancient proverb from the bible says this:

You shall know the truth and the truth will set you free.

Let's look at how this plays out in our search for God's existence.

SHOOT THE MESSENGER PLEASE!

People who look to the bible for answers are often repelled, not from what is written, but from what is taught based on what is written. The conclusions gleaned from these ancient pages are often untenable with the present world we live in.

Three of the most egregious qualities ascribed to God are commonly called the *omnis*.

- God is omniscient (all-knowing).
- God is omnipresent (all-present).
- God is omnipotent (all-powerful).

To these, let's add a fourth commonly held assumption:

- God is in control of everything.

Many of our definitions of God come from these ideas. It is also from these attributes that people hurl charges at God:

- Why did God allow the volcano to erupt?
- Why didn't God warn me about the car in my blind spot?
- Why didn't God stop that banker who stole my mother's life savings?

Yet people are basing their accusations on definitions of God's nature…definitions that may or may not be true.

So, here it is:

- Is God all-knowing?
- Is God everywhere?
- Is God all-powerful?
- Is God in control of everything?

Keep in mind that we are talking about our experiences of a God who may or may not be here on earth. God may very well be something different, something more, in another realm. Is it possible that to relate to human beings, God assumes a role that is relatable? Isn't it reasonable to expect him to function in a world of his making (assuming he is the creator) according to the laws governing that world? Most likely, he would take on a role on earth that does not violate the laws of our existence—most notably, our free will.

OK, that's a lot of supposition in one paragraph. Let's make this a bit more relevant.

ANNA

I have a four-year-old granddaughter, Anna. When I'm at my full stature, I tower above her. When Anna wants to play, however, I get down on the floor with her. She loves it when I'm sitting or lying on my side. She looks straight into me with those baby blues and pretty much writes a blank check on my soul.

When we play, it's usually a game of her contrivance requiring leaps of imagination that I'm not accustomed to. But it delights me to see her agile mind bound from one fantasy to another, weaving a story that shows a grasp of reality beyond my everyday experience. Anna takes me on journeys to places I did not know existed.

That's the joy of her.

Sure, I could scatter the block castles she's created with a slight of my hand. Her Legos could be crushed under my feet. I could dismiss her claims that the building at the end of the driveway is a dragon's lair and that we have to rescue a princess.

But what of it? I'm bigger, but she's the builder. I'm wiser, but she's the learner. I've been to the garage a thousand times, but to her, it's a hero's land to explore and conquer. I'm the adult, but it's her childhood. And someday, she'll choose my nursing home.

Could God be like that? Could God delight in being at our level, hearing our stories, sharing in our discoveries, watching us grow? Could the superpowered God shed his cape long enough to walk where we walk, share our lives and engender relationships, conveying all that naturally flows from a portal of openness: trust, compassion, caring, strength, insight and purpose?

Does the construct of free will—the environment we seem to find ourselves in—require that God not violate it without destroying what he created? Think about it. Without free will, what are we? Slaves? Machines? Rocks with hair?

Without free will, we are inanimate objects leading a directionless existence while awaiting the input of our master whose rudimentary direction is all that keeps us alive.

"Breath in. Breath out. Breath In. Breath out. Coffee break. OK, back to work. Breath in...."

This is not who we are. Therefore, this cannot be who God is.

THE BOOKS

Of course, if the bible says otherwise, we do well to consider this collection of books as containing some evidence of God's existence. At the very least, we should consider its perspective.

So, what do we read about this God whom many consider knows everything, controls everything and can do anything?

Well, a prophet named Jeremiah quotes God as saying:

They [the Jewish people] have built the high places of Baal to burn their children in the fire as offerings to Baal—something I did not command or mention, nor did it enter my mind.

"Nor did it enter my mind…" Interesting phrase to describe a God that people say knows everything. Obviously, God in this story is not pleased in this scene, so why didn't he stop it, assuming he is all-powerful? For that matter, if he's everywhere, why was he surprised at all? Is this a statement from a God who knows all, can do all, is everywhere and controls everything? Huh…

But wait! There's more!

From the book of Genesis, at a pivotal moment in the history of the Jewish people, we read of the patriarch Abraham who is told by God to sacrifice his son Isaac. In obedience, Abraham prepares him as a sacrifice on an altar. Yet as the knife intended for the heart of all he loves is arcing through the air, God hollers "STOP!"

As dramatic as this moment is, it's God's next words to Abraham, as recorded in Genesis, that carry the weight of all that will come afterward.

"Now I know that you fear God, because you have not withheld from me your son, your only son."

Now, I ask you: Is a God who says "Now I know…" a God who knows everything? If God knew *now*, did he know it *before now?* Apparently not.

So, can we say that the God of the bible knows everything? No, we can't say that. If he is in control, why does he have to test people? And if he is all-powerful, why does he need people at all?

97

What is it that God apparently doesn't know? Well, from these two verses, he doesn't always know what people will choose. Sometimes, their choices surprise him. Other times, their choices prove something to him.

Can you see, though, how this description of God flows with free will? If we are free to choose, then we are *free* indeed. The future, at least in the microcosm of our lives against the backdrop of the infinite universe, is influenced by what we decide. This is what God—if he exists—granted us when we were created with free will.

Some believers in God will argue to the contrary. Their definition of God requires that he know everything, be everywhere and be all-powerful, because how else can he control everything?

There's an escapable conclusion to this discordant data set. It appears that God—as defined by the biblical evidence—is not in control, is not all-powerful, is not everywhere and does not know everything. It's when our faulty definitions cause us to stop seeking God that there's a problem evaluating the evidence.

My granddaughter Anna doesn't have to know everything about me to relate to me. She can think I hung the moon or invented air. I don't care. I want her to know the basics: I exist. I love her. I want to be with her. And I'm the smartest guy on the planet. Oh, and if we get around to it...my name is Grandpa.

If the omnis cause you to reject the idea of God as portrayed by some students of the bible, take heart. There are other points of view, definitions that make a little more sense. With a bit of research, you will arrive at the source of these misconceptions and be able to discard them. Intelligent, well-meaning people struggle to define God amidst a sea of evidence, but they are seeking truth. People just like you.

You'll know the truth when you find it, and that truth will set you free. You'll identify the truth by the freedom it engenders. Which begs another definition. What is freedom, anyway?

FREEDOM

Freedom is an interesting concept that everyone thinks about but few understand. So, here's an illustration to confuse you even more.

In a story from the bible, a long-haired strong man— the strongest guy on the known earth—spends his time roaming the countryside, fighting the villainous Philistines who oppress his people, the Jews. Incidentally, this guy is not just strong. He is supernaturally strong. It's his superpower. And because of it, he is free to do anything he feels like doing, which is mostly roaming the countryside and beating up these idiots intent on harassing his people.

Fed up with losing to this guy, the Philistines devise a plan to trap him. It seems that this strong man is enamored with the lovely tresses, subtle fragrance and soft bed of a fair maiden in yonder land, so they contract her to discover the secret of his strength.

As he lies in her arms, love-drunk on her passions, she whispers her query. "What is the secret of your strength, my love?"

He mumbles something about binding him with cords and he would not be able to break it. Armed with this information, she ties him up as he slumbers, and when he wakes, she cries: "The Philistines are upon you!"

He instantly breaks the cords and sets out after the imaginary foe as she decries his deception. "Come on, what's the real source of your power?"

So, he tries another story. Vines. But he breaks those too. On and on it goes as he feeds her one lie after another: rope, chain, kryptonite, and she realizes she's being duped. One might wonder if he is enjoying a tad too much the means she employs to lure him to his destruction. But nothing can restrain him. Indeed, nothing in life has ever impeded his ability to do whatever he wanted to do.

At her rope's end, she throws a fit and retreats behind a wall of silence. Ah, the classic maneuver. And the lovesick puppy breaks down and tells her the truth.

"It's my hair. Cut it and I'm just like every other bald guy yipping at the moon and wishing the sun weren't so hot."

So, she loves him up and shaves him while he sleeps, then calls her Philistine employers. They bind him with the strongest rope they can find. When he awakes, surrounded by his severed locks, he tries to break free and can't. "Arrrrggghhhhh!!" he cries, but to no avail. They gouge out his eyes and strap him to a grinding wheel, mocking him from a distance.

The man who killed us by the thousands is no more.

He now understands freedom, having lost it.

So, what is truth? Truth is what brings freedom. How do we know we are free? If I sit still, am I free to move? I won't know until I attempt to move. How free am I? Well, I only know that by how far I am able to go.

Am I free to think? Speak my mind? Explore ideas? I don't know until I try and others argue with me, trying to change my mind or shut me down.

How far can I really go in anything? And what increases my range?

If a salesperson says these new Nikes will double my distance, how will I know until I try?

Truth. Freedom. Range of motion. We call ourselves free, but how far do we test that freedom?

In our story, the bald guy finally got his revenge. The Philistines were so consumed with their victory dance that they forgot that hair eventually grows back. The strong guy found his strength and destroyed the people that enslaved him. That's when he learned true freedom.

Until you try something new, something purported to bring freedom, you'll never know how free you are.

The ancient books of the bible are supposed to be based on the truth about God and man. Maybe they are; maybe they're not. But until you try, you'll never know, will you?

How free are you?

12

Chain Reaction

PEOPLE'S INTERPRETATION of certain bible passages is not the only place we find obstructions to the truth of God's existence. Far from it. In our modern age, there is reason aplenty to dissuade one of God's existence. One such area of thinking involves the idea that man is a god unto themselves. Curiously, a phrase from the bible is misquoted to support this idea.

The kingdom of God is within you.

This is how it is quoted in the book of Luke. However, this phrase presents a few problems to the purveyors of a godless existence. First, it refers to God—kind of a non-starter to many folks. Making matters worse, it attributes to this God a kingdom, as if he's in charge of something.

No worries. A selective snip here and a tuck there and *voila*! We have the new quote just in time to save our prickling skins.

The kingdom is within you.

Now we have a kingdom, and by definition, a kingdom must have a king, but since it's within us with no other ruler referenced, who's left to be king? We are! Joy to the world, the savior reigns. And that savior is...us!

Adherents to this idea cite the immediate freedom it conveys. No longer constrained by a dark religion, they can shed their hairshirts in favor of silks and skinny jeans. They are free. They can go anywhere they choose. Do whatever they like. Nothing holds them back. No oppression. No deformity of conformity. They call it free-living, and it sustains them...for a while. They are free from the idea of anything beyond themselves.

Note, however, the key phrase: *the idea.*

If God exists, and yet people revel in a life assuming God doesn't exist, then it would be incorrect to say they are free from anything beyond themselves. In fact, they are only free from *the idea* of anything beyond themselves.

Ideas are powerful. Long before anything actually enslaves us or emancipates us, there is an idea germinating to action. Bad ideas enslave people. Good ideas free people.

REVOLUTION

When the idea of God's possible existence invades a non-believer's consciousness, it can be disruptive, even revolutionary. Everything changes as the thought string slowly untangles. It looks something like this.

If God exists, then:

Something greater than I exists.

How big is this God?

What does this God know of me?

What does this God want of me?

How does this God feel about me?

What can I get from this God?

What do I owe this God?

With serious consideration of God's existence, the center of our universe shifts and everything we love and fear now resides in dimensions beyond our carefully crafted paradigms. What of our lives, our loved ones, our plans, our needs? Everything that once drove us down the road in the morning and brought us back at eventide is now laid bare on the altar of the possible existence of this supreme being.

Discomfort is understandable. We are hierarchal creatures. We relate to one another in degrees. Rank is formed, acquired and honored in all walks of life regardless of our professed egalitarianism. No one is equal to another. We all have bosses and subordinates, people and circumstances we are in charge of or who are in charge of us. The IRS is over us, but we go to the polls to elect its leaders. Our children are our charges, but a three-year-old can rule the roost with a tantrum. Our friends love us, but we know who is on top, who is at the bottom, who has more sway than others. When five guys get together to decide where to go for the evening, leaders emerge, decisions are made and the rest follow. It's natural. It's who we are—communal beings following and leading.

In the midst of this consideration of a higher being, our hierarchical schemes collapse like a house of cards. Life is never going to be the same if we acknowledge the existence of a God who transcends every structure we've ever bowed our knee to: the family, the workplace, the social circles, fantasy football. It's all upended by this new kid who shows up wanting to play. And oh, by the way, he carries a nifty football. It's game on, but what rules does he play by?

Nothing will ever be the same and we know it. That is why we delay with such determination the mere consideration of this God's existence...until we acquire some knowledge of his possible nature.

THE REAL ISSUE

The struggle, it seems, is not in wondering if God exists. Rather, it's in *sensing* that God exists. In some intangible way, we all sense that God, in some form or fashion, exists. We do. It's the questions that come next that vex us. It's what happens when we face what we sense is true.

So, I'm not in charge?

So, my life is under God?

What if he screws it all up for me?

Maybe he already has.

Can I trust him?

How does he feel about me?

Put plainly, if there is stuff, is there not a stuff maker? There must be a being who made the sunsets and the waterfalls, the songs of lovers, the earth yielding to the farmer, the sky beckoning the aviator and the sea luring the sailor.

Yes, we live in a world of abundance and yet we encounter lack. We live in a world of wonder and yet we find destruction and despair. We live largely in peace and yet find war. And one more thing. We live in a world sensing God but resisting the implications of his existence.

Could there be a connection?

13

Good and Evil

MOST PEOPLE WHO CLAIM to have a relationship with God cite one overwhelming characteristic of this God. Now, these are not simply people who cling to a few bible passages in a momentary panic. Rather, they are veterans of a life believing in God, people who have lived their belief in good times and bad, who have entered the valley of the shadow of death and come out whole on the other end.

They attest that there is only one aspect of God—one unifying trait that makes his entry the event they longed for their entire lives. It is the catalyst that assured them that his presence would not destroy all that they had built but would instead transform everything they loved into that which they could only dream of.

He loves them.

To hear these people tell it, all that we love, he loves more. We love our kids; so does he. We love our marriages; so does he. Our homes, our songs, our professions...everywhere we direct our energy, he waits to make our best better.

As if this wasn't enough, we are told one more thing.

He is good.

Could it be that our resistance to God is a lack of assurance of these two things: that God loves us and that he is good?

If I am engaged to be married and am understandably nervous about such an arrangement, would it not go better if I knew with certainty that my future spouse loves me and is good? I mean, I'm ready to throw my life wide open to a perfect stranger, someone I only think I know, regardless of how long I've known them. In reality, however, we can never know someone until we fully open our life to them. I'll never know how they cook until I let them into my kitchen. Not just my appliances or sink, but my prize spices, my clippings of herbs and spices, my dusty bottles of spirits and wines, my dogeared copy of *Joy of Cooking*.

OK, so maybe they can't make a decent marinara sauce, but do they love me? And are they good?

I have a friend who describes it this way: Accepting God's existence is like the glance of future lovers across a crowded room, the chance meeting of an old friend on a crowded street, hearing a baby's first laugh, throwing open windows in Spring. It's the beginning of a new life, and it changes everything. To these folks, God is love. Are they right?

CONFLICT

If God is good, then the evidence for his existence is everywhere, in the best of circumstances and in the worst.

When John Steinbeck closed his seminal work, *The Grapes of Wrath*, he left us with the image of a young mother who comes upon a dying man. She's just lost her baby, a casualty of the abject poverty afflicting her family during the Great Depression of the 1930s. But she is still lactating and the man is starving to death. She puts everyone else out of the room, kneels down and begins to nurse him.

Yes, there is horror in the world. Most people can accept this as evidence of evil's existence. But to point them to the goodness in the world and call it evidence of good's existence is a more difficult case to make.

What if the conflict we see around us is not the *reign* of evil or the absence of good, but the *invasion* of good upon the evil in the world?

Think about it. If evil alone existed, would there be conflict? Of course not. Conflict is about challenge, differences, opposing forces. If there was only evil in the world, what would challenge evil? What would rise up to fight it? It's only when good is present that conflict ensues.

Consider recent history.

A hundred years ago, Irish peasants were starving and being pushed off the land by feudal landlords intent on making a buck elsewhere. Today, Ireland is different. Certainly not without its struggles, but the economic system that enslaved people no longer exists. The conditions under which people starved have been changed. Things got better. Good won over evil.

In this mindset, conflict is not evidence of the absence of good but evidence the presence of good. Wars are fought over differences. There are no wars where there is agreement. The evil in the headlines is being disrupted by the good in the world, even if the disruption is merely the reporting of the evil.

Germany was instrumental in starting two world wars, conflicts that fostered atrocities unparalleled in human history. Not just the holocaust, but the ravages of the Soviet army on Europe's armies and civilians and the untold millions who were victims of the armaments unleashed by all sides.

Today, Germany is at peace with its neighbors and is the economic engine that holds together the rest of the European Union. Good won over evil.

Japan unleashed a swath of terror and savagery across the Pacific. Atrocities such as the Rape of Nanking showed how depraved mankind can be. Today, Japan is at peace with the world and is a leader in economic and technological advancement. Good won over evil.

What of our modern perpetrators? What of Russia, China, Iran and North Korea? What of the insidious corruptors of our societies—opioids, oppression, greed, disease, racism and terrorism? Let history be our teacher. Where there is evil, good arises. Where good arises, there is conflict. Where there is conflict, good wins.

If God is good, and there is goodness in the world, then is God in the world?

The evidence of good in all its forms: love, caring, prosperity, healing, forgiveness, understanding and fulfillment, is all around us. We can't mistake it, yet we can ignore it by acquiring the habit of blindness and joining the ranks of those who march through darkness with one hand on the back of the sightless guide before them.

14

Change Not

THERE IS A NOTION that says God never changes, that he is immovable. People pull this idea from the bible, among other sources.

> *For I am the Lord; I change not.*

> Malachi 3:6 KJV

> *Jesus Christ is the same yesterday and today and forever.*

> Hebrews 13:8 KJV

Now, that's certainly true from a logical standpoint. A thing is what it is, right? If I hand you an apple, it's not going to magically reappear as an orange, unless we're at some magic show where the guy makes playing cards appear on the inside of car windows. (That guy creeps me out.)

So, we can say that God does not change. But herein lies the rub. If you think wrong information can cause confusion, wait until you try the truth.

Saying something is true does not define it. We can know something is true and still spend the rest of our lives understanding it.

It is true that my spouse loves me. I know it's true. But do I understand it? Like when I stand in front of the mirror and face my shortcomings; when I fail to make her smile; when she sputters "You don't listen," and I reply, "What'd you say?"

It's true that she loves me, but for the life of me, I don't get it. I'd have left me years ago. (I tried once, but they treated me for schizophrenia and we've been together ever since.)

It seems logical that God does not change fundamentally—a being is what it is—yet what does it mean to not change? As in all things, it's the definition that drives the interpretation.

Often, adherents to particular theology (a belief about God) will latch onto a particular view of God—perhaps that he's a righteous God—and they go on to define *righteous* as "demanding payment for sin" just as in the Old Testament days. And when you try to offer a different view of *righteous*, one developed in the 21st century, they retort: "God does not change!"

You know what they're really saying? They're saying *their definition* of God does not change. In fact, they are declaring that their theology is not going to change, period. In so doing, they have just violated an important principle of truth: Our understanding of truth is constantly evolving.

"My present understanding is this..."

Harold Eberle

What if an aspect of God's nature is that he's constantly changing? What if he, like his creation, is evolving, growing, dying, rising, expanding, breathing, sighing, expanding and contracting? What if God is all these things? Is he still God?

What if God responds to the demands put on him just like we do? When my kids need cash and they catch me in a charitable mood, they make their case and my heart melts. I hand over my wallet and say, "Just leave the driver's license."

Could God be like that?

What if I'm feeling like the dumbest guy on earth? Perhaps I'm trying to figure out how to open an email app designed by a 12-year-old in a dank basement in Calcutta who became an overnight billionaire when IBM bought his software company. Then a friend comes by seeking advice. I may not feel that I have anything to offer, but I can listen. People need to be listened to. So, I put down my tools and give him my full attention. Hearing his difficulties, my heart quickly melts. Soon, wisdom for his situation floods my soul and I give him the benefit of everything I've learned in the past 100 years (give or take a decade). Suddenly I'm the sage oracle who, an hour ago, was the village idiot.

What caused this transformation? His need awakened my supply. It took me out of a mindset where I knew nothing, and into a mindset where I have a bit more experience. Compassion was the prime mover in my shift from dummy to demigod.

Could God be like that?

Say I walk into a bank and look around. What do I see? Piles of cash? Gold bullion? No. Just harried tellers wondering what squirrelly problem I'm bringing them today. Yet I know they have my money because I gave it to them last month, and the month before that, and all the months for the past several years. Now I want some of it back so I can buy a new power tool. So, I give the nice teller a slip of paper, show some I.D., and walk out with cash that was not visible when I entered.

Could God be like that?

Now, to the distant observer of these scenarios, I was both uncharitable and charitable, dumb and wise, broke and wealthy (until I got to Home Depot). This observer might say that I change a lot. And I do. But here's the kicker...follow me here.

I'm still me.

Even though I changed on one level, the big picture is that I'm still the same person.

For I am the Jim; I change not.

\- Jim

Make sense?

SURPRISED BY GOD

Concerning our perceptions of God as evidence of his existence, is it possible that we all perceive of God differently, that the God you experience and believe in is vastly different from the God that I believe in?

Different...but the same? Who is this God who can be moved based on our belief in his ability to meet our needs? Is it possible that the aspects of God vary with our faith in his nature, but he's the same God?

You may look at someone else's *God* and say "That's a load of crap. I never want or need a God like that."

And you know what? You're right. You don't need a God like that. You need a God who relates to you and yours—a God who meets your needs.

What if God is relational? What if he relates to us individually? Assuming he is the creator of the universe, everything he made is relational. Even our measurement system, based on the physical laws of the universe, is relational.

(OK, the speed of light...you got me there. Just work with me here!)

15

Simple Thanks

I HAVE A FRIEND who rejects God's existence. She says, "Everything's fine in my life. Why do I need God?"

See, she relates to God on a need-basis, yet to her perception, she doesn't need anything. She has all she needs just the way things are. So why bother with God?

Of course, that begs the argument: *Well then, how about a simple 'Thanks!' to the creator of the universe, the source of all you have?*

But her definition of God doesn't include being the source of all she has. So, to suggest that she thank this being that she isn't even remotely interested in is foolishness to her.

I mention her because she's not alone.

In Western culture—I don't know what it's like for other religions—people are invited into Christianity on the basis of "Look what a mess your life is. Come to God and he'll clean it up for you."

And for years, this has worked...for drug addicts and alcoholics, thieves and murders, the lonely, the broken, the forgotten, the loveless, the huddled masses yearning to breathe free.

It hasn't worked so well for those who are none of these things. There is a segment of the population that is doing just fine without any professed acknowledgement of God. And without a definition that includes God as the source of all they have, there is no reason for these people to pursue a relationship with God, until...

...things go really, really wrong. Or things go really, really right.

Sometimes we are in a forest searching for fossil records of the last known dinosaur, when suddenly the earth shifts. What we thought was a boulder turns out to be a toenail, and before us, a thousand feet tall, stands the majestic lizard that we thought had perished eons ago. And she's looking for lunch. Fortunately, she only eats plants. (Thankfully, we packed a change of clothes.)

There is always something to be thankful for.

This is the best of times and the worst of times. So what else is new? The bad news is that the Martians have landed in Manhattan, and have checked in at the Waldorf-Astoria. The good news is that they only eat homeless people and they pee gasoline.

Kurt Vonnegut, *Armageddon in Retrospect*

There are times when the godless life we thought was just fine turns out to be so richly blessed that in acknowledging it, we are brought to our knees in gratitude.

If there is a God who created this world, might we not direct some of our gratitude in that direction?

C. S. Lewis, author of many famous Christian works, was a contemporary of J. R. R. Tolkien. They met at Oxford, England, and forged a deep friendship. At the time, Tolkien was a Christian and Lewis was an atheist. However, Lewis was influenced through his friendship with Tolkien and also by the writings of G. K. Chesterton.

Lewis described his conversion to Christianity, saying he vigorously resisted conversion and was brought into Christianity like a prodigal, "kicking, struggling, resentful, and darting his eyes in every direction for a chance to escape."

He described his struggle in his later book, *Surprised by Joy*:

> You must picture me alone in that room in Magdalen [College, Oxford], night after night, feeling, whenever my mind lifted even for a second from my work, the steady, unrelenting approach of Him whom I so earnestly desired not to meet. That which I greatly feared had at last come upon me. In the Trinity Term of 1929 I gave in, and admitted that God was God, and knelt and prayed: perhaps, that night, the most dejected and reluctant convert in all England.

His conversion is remarkable for what it contains as well as what it does not contain. It does not contain the story of a hardscrabble life ripped to shreds by hate and paranoia, an alien to all who dared love him, a smackhead strung out on a host of pharmaceuticals and skipping bail hearings. These are common threads to religious conversions in our modern society, but based on Lewis' experience, being a broken wretch is not a requirement for the acknowledgment of God's existence.

Lewis had many things going well in his life. He held academic positions in English literature at both Oxford University and Cambridge University. He was an expert in his field. The profound change in his life was, as he said, "admitting that God was God."

Admitting that God was God.

It is a mistake to expect to be flogged into accepting the awareness of God.

You may not need bailing out. You may not need your marriage restored or your kids rescued from drugs. Your bank account might be just fine and your cars might start every time you press the button. Life could genuinely be outstanding, even peachy keen.

What you need, however, is a deeper understanding of what you have and how you got it. We live in a world that is gradually coming to grips with the idea that negative forces such as hate, war, greed and ignorance are not beneficial to our mutual prosperity; that those things that aid the whole in turn aid the individual. Indeed, society is turning to more positive approaches to relating to one another and seeking each other's well-being. In so doing, evidence of God's existence is emerging in an unexpected way.

THANK YOU

Amazon—love them or hate them—knows that if they mistreat their customers, they'll lose them. Medical service providers realize that patients who feel misunderstood by doctors and nurses quickly lose patience with the organization and go elsewhere. Hotels bend over backward to please their customers. Surveys of customer satisfaction are now commonplace after a night's stay. Lines of inquiry are:

Thank you for your business.

How were you treated?

Would you recommend us to a friend?

Did you feel well-cared for?

Would you please return the towels?

Such simple-sounding outreaches are revolutionizing how we treat each other in the marketplace and how we expect to be treated. As bad as some places in the world appear to be, there is evidence that the world is getting better.

Remember, I started this section talking about people who are doing so well that they don't see the need for God. Please consider this logic. It is contradictory to say that

a) we don't need God

b) the world is going to hell.

Obviously, some people's worlds are not going to hell. Might God—in the form of love and goodness—have something to do with the improvement?

Where do positive-based methods come from? Where do we get the idea that treating people well—as opposed to abusing them—is the key to getting the best they have to offer…for us and for them? Where do we learn that feeding our neighbors when they are hungry ensures that the community that sustains all of us remains healthy and viable?

Consider these thoughts.

Love your neighbor as yourself.

A righteous man knows the rights of the poor; a wicked man does not understand such knowledge.

If you pour yourself out for the hungry and satisfy the desire of the afflicted, then shall your light rise in the darkness and your gloom be as the noonday.

Let the thief no longer steal, but rather let him labor, doing honest work with his own hands, so that he may have something to share with anyone in need.

These teachings and more are from the collection of books we call the bible, that eclectic amalgamation of man's yearning for God and God's yearning for man, written thousands of years ago. It's not the only book to espouse these values, but it's one of them.

People are discovering that treating others in all walks of life—business, marriage, education, community—is mutually beneficial. Yes, exceptions exist. The fact that we all know of the exceptions, however, means that they are viewed as abnormal. Two hundred years ago, people accepted a sweatshop environment as the norm in manufacturing. Today…not so much. One hundred and sixty years ago, we fought a war over slavery. Today, slavery is anathema to people's worldview, even if vestiges of it are still being dealt with.

What if God exists? What if this God is good? What if people who know him shared their experiences, not just in the collection of books called the bible, but in all media available to them at the time?

Would you listen? Would you consider God as the source to all the good that you have?

If God exists, and he is good, and he loves us, then we owe it to him and ourselves to explore this relationship...if for no other reason than out of gratitude.

It could start with a simple *thank-you*.

16

Last Call

WHAT WILL WE ACCEPT as evidence of God's existence?

If we define God as love, and we find love in the world, is that evidence that God exists?

If we define God as just, and we find justice in the world, is that evidence that God exists?

If we define God in a variety of ways and we find these ways in the world, is that evidence that God exists?

I can't argue that the negatives don't exist. We all know they do. But consider the simple metaphor of light. Darkness exists, but so does light. I can let darkness define my observations, or I can define it by light.

No doubt, everything I've written on these pages can be refuted a dozen times over. I have arguments, others have counter-arguments. We could go on forever playing "Oh yeah? What about this? What about that?" It might be fun for a while, but it'll get us nowhere.

The mind—our logical nature—can conjure up a host of perspectives. That's the beauty of the thing. It can imagine limitless possibilities and it despises confinement. For every reason to accept the possibility of God's existence, it will find many more reasons to think otherwise.

Thinking is great, and admittedly, my appeal thus far has been pitched to those acquainted with the practice. Yet there is another way to encounter evidence of God's existence—*experience*. It is a place where something moves within us and we know...we just know...that we have encountered something greater than ourselves...something we don't understand.

Sometimes, the mind leads us flawlessly, and sometimes the mind is like a kid playing in a sandbox. It's more fun to toss sand into the air than it is to settle down and actually build something.

An encounter with God is described just that—actually doing something. It's when the mind is temporarily bypassed and the heart is flooded with the presence of something it has only dreamed of, something we cannot do on our own. This is what is meant by these proverbs:

> *You will seek me and find me when you seek me with all your heart.*

> *Come near to God and he will come near to you.*

WITNESS

A friend of mine, who grew up in a horrific environment, found himself walking the streets as a teenage prostitute. He was selling his body, not out of hunger in the conventional sense but from a hunger for love. He was desperate for someone to demonstrate kindness toward him, to find value in him, if only for a few moments. He was spiraling out of control and wanted to stop but there were no handholds. He'd tried suicide several times.

One evening, he stumbled into a church service and opened his heart to the God that the preacher was talking about—a God of compassion, forgiveness and love. Here's what he says happened next:

> I cannot express the feeling at that moment. All I can say is Jesus touched me. I cried with all my heart, asking forgiveness of all my sins and receiving the same. In an instant, I became a new man. I was filled with love. I was healed!

> I went home that night with a smile on my face and a joyful heart. I was never the same since.

Today, he works with youth on the same streets that nearly took his life.

Here is an experience of missionary friends I know who spent 10 years in Uruguay. This is their description of working with a local diplomatic couple.

> For six weeks, my husband and I met with a Uruguayan diplomatic couple who were generational atheists. They were born and raised that way and proud of it. During those six weeks, we taught on relational brain skills and how to share emotions to build joy in their relationship and family. We never mentioned God or Jesus, although they knew we were Christians.

> At the end of the six weeks, I asked for their impressions of the work we did with them.

131

The woman broke down in tears and confessed, "I have to say, I was born an atheist, raised atheist. However, I can no longer deny the existence of God because I feel him. I feel him giving me joy. There is some force outside of me that is glad to be with me, and I can only imagine it is God. So, this week, I gave myself to this 'other' force."

I was amazed! Just by helping them feel valued and enjoyed, somehow, she could feel God and no longer denied his existence.

I found that all of my Uruguayan friends who were atheists were so because this feeling of joy was outside of their experience. No amount of logical explanation could sway them. For them, God, if he existed, was something to be experienced. Their decision to not believe was never based in intellectual or rational thought, but on a deeper void. When God reached them there, they had the evidence they needed to believe.

There are millions of such stories. We can believe them or not. We can take them at face value or read into them any manner of rationalization. Here's the simple point. If even one of these stories is accurate in saying that something called God changed someone, then that is evidence of God's existence as he is defined.

The evidence of a positive will always take precedence over the lack of evidence supporting a negative. One vote vs. zero votes wins the election. Exceptions will always exist. But normal also exists. The mind can theorize until the sun sets and comes up the other side, but experience can only be acknowledged or denied. The truth is, God needs no introduction; he only needs an opening. You will know when you encounter the living God. It's that clear.

Normal is rising.

17

The Great Gamble

IF YOU WANT TO KNOW if God exists, look within yourself. Not in the headlines or the words to the latest soul-lament set to music, but to the one territory that you can attest to with authority—yourself.

Ask yourself what that landscape looks like. What do you see? What do you like? What don't you like? What are you pleased with? Proud of? And what do you wish you could change?

Then recall our earlier discussion that a search for God follows the pattern of our needs and desires. If you think about it, they are there because we cannot satisfy them in our present state.

Our needs and desires will lead us on a search for God if we are willing to take a gamble and approach him, opening our hearts and focus on what we know of him. It is not uncommon for prayers and meditations to start with "God, if you are there, please...." The words don't matter. It's the focus of the heart that matters—the approach, the attitude, the flow of energy seeking God himself. Not the hand of God, but the heart of God. Not what he can give, but who he is.

Deep within us is a desire for relationship. We know this through our needs, wants and drives, not just for material things but for deeper things—a sense that we are not alone, that we have a purpose beyond our daily existence, that life is eternal, that everything we love has a destiny, that our dreams are real, that the shadows have life, that the symphony we've heard since childhood is from an orchestra with one seat reserved for us.

Relationship is like that. We hunger for something beyond ourselves, something we cannot supply on our own. So, off we go seeking it.

God's great gamble is that he gave us a free will. Thus, we might seek the answer to our needs elsewhere without him. Or we might find our needs met by him but attribute this to something else entirely.

We'll discover a friend and revel in their companionship, ascribing to luck the serendipitous events that brought us together.

We'll seek fulfillment fighting for social justice, neglecting the source of the universal absolutes that bring peace and harmony.

We'll find meaning through spiritual encounters, attributing the power of metaphysics to an amorphous universe.

We'll discover the beauty of the natural world and look no further than the laws of nature, overlooking the greater search for the author of the beauty.

We'll seek inner peace, choosing to frame a personal kingdom within us, ignoring the evidence that we are not sufficient gods unto ourselves.

God's great gamble is that he made us as he is. So, when we look within ourselves, we see his qualities and have a choice to make. We can say those qualities are ours alone. Or we can say those qualities are evidence of God living with us.

The God of the bible is a God deeply entwined with his creation. He is described not as aloof but integral, not hiding but in plain sight. If this is true, then the question of his existence becomes an issue of our perception. If God is all around us, is it possible we have become inured to the distinction between what is God and what is ourselves?

Perhaps. Brew a cup of tea and determine what is tea and what is water.

We have a free will to sift through the evidence, to decide what we will accept as evidence of God's existence. The choice—as in all freewill-based systems—is ours. Nobody is going to make it for us. Yet if we believe what others believe because of who they are, we have surrendered our free will by letting them do our thinking for us.

Make up your own mind. Own your feelings. Be led by your inner compass. And consider the evidence around you.

About the Author

I have been writing and editing for over 20 years. I make my home in Sharpsburg, Maryland, at the edge of the Antietam Battlefield. I'm a Navy veteran, a retired engineer and a publisher.

I welcome any and all comments—technical, theological, or "Get a life, Bryson!" I enjoy discourse with people...until they become annoying. You can annoy me here at: JamesLBryson@gmail.com.

(Please, feel free to contact me.)

Some recent books you might enjoy that I have been a part of, either as author, ghostwriter or editor:

- ➤ *The Real Deal – The Life, Death and Resurrection of Robert Clayborn Nash,* by Jim Bryson
- ➤ *Relational Authority, Authentic Leadership,* by Clay Nash
- ➤ *Activating the Prophetic,* by Clay Nash
- ➤ *Hope For Nerds,* by Harold Eberle
- ➤ *Between Mountains – Finding God in Valleys,* by Dr. Tony Lewis

Made in the USA
Monee, IL
10 November 2021

81697016R00085